"From the Dan Dan Lasagna to the Mapo Paneer, the recipes in *Kung Food* are so vibrant and bursting with flavor that you'll want to scrape your plates clean—but it's Jon's wonderful writing that gives new meaning to what it means to be Chinese American."
—Andy Baraghani, author of *The Cook You Want to Be*

"*Kung Food* is one of those cookbooks that makes you want to *sprint* to the kitchen, book tucked tightly under your arm. Much like in his videos, Jon mixes heart, culture, an encyclopedic knowledge of spices, and good freaking food in a way that'll make you excited to try everything. Also, thanks to this book my wok is properly seasoned for the *first time ever*. Can't recommend enough!"
—Alexis Nikole Nelson, James Beard Award–winning content creator and food writer

"*Kung Food* flings open the gates to cultural cuisine and invites all of us to a stunning and sumptuous meal of delicious food and powerful storytelling, as well as Jon's joyous pursuit of home cooking."
—Joanne Lee Molinaro, *New York Times* bestselling author of *The Korean Vegan*

"Jon has captured the delicious complexities of being a third-culture kid and made me feel proud to consider myself one. His recipes feel at once nostalgic and novel, and at the same time they will teach us how to be a better and more adventurous home cook."
—Kristina Cho, James Beard Award–winning author of *Mooncakes and Milk Bread*

"Jon offers a progressive and deeply creative take on Chinese American cooking while simultaneously inspiring us to pay homage to our collective food histories."
—DeVonn Francis of Yardy World

"Jon will thirst trap you into a sensory journey celebrating the complexity of Chinese and American flavors. The industry cook in me wants to keep reading. Such a stunning and functional book."
—Matt Broussard, @ACookNamedMatt

Kung Food

Jon Kung

Kung Food

Chinese American Recipes from a Third-Culture Kitchen

Photographs by Johnny Miller

Clarkson Potter/Publishers
New York

Published in the United States by Clarkson Potter/
Publishers, an imprint of the Crown Publishing Group, a
division of Penguin Random House LLC, New York.
ClarksonPotter.com

CLARKSON POTTER is a trademark and POTTER with
colophon is a registered trademark of Penguin Random
House LLC.

Library of Congress Cataloging-in-Publication Data has
been applied for.

ISBN 978-0-593-57817-9
Ebook ISBN 978-0-593-57818-6

Printed in China

Photographer: Johnny Miller
Designer: Su Barber
Editor: Raquel Pelzel
Editorial assistant: Bianca Cruz
Creative director: Marysarah Quinn
Production editor: Joyce Wong
Production manager: Philip Leung
Compositors: Merri Ann Morrell and Hannah Hunt
Food stylist: Rebecca Jurkevich
Prop stylist: Sarah Smart
Recipe testers: Sarah Dickerman, Elizabeth Bossin,
Grace Rosanova, and Danielle DeLott
Copy editor: Ivy McFadden
Indexer: Elizabeth Parson
Marketer: Chloe Aryeh

10 9 8 7 6 5 4 3 2 1

First Edition

For Bubs

Contents

Recipes

Introduction

Third culture is the celebration of the in-between.

When people define themselves as "third-culture" kids, they're usually referring to their experience as the children of immigrants or expats—those of us who grew up both in the culture of their parents' country (in my case, Hong Kong) and the culture of the adopted country (US and Canada). As a third-culture kid, I grew up neither fully here nor there— I didn't feel completely accepted as American or Chinese. Personally, I see "third culture" as being something that is inclusive and full of possibility. It has had a huge influence on art, literature, fashion, and design, and I would argue that it can also apply to food. I would describe my culinary style as American Chinese, or Third-Culture Chinese, and really what does that mean but to celebrate my own expression of cultural diversity where I live now? The American Culinary Renaissance that we saw in the 2010s brought a great affirmation of many countries' diversity to what would be called New American restaurants. It was just the American acceptance of the ingredients of many of its cultural communities in one place (usually a place with lots of Edison bulbs). My third-cultural Chinese and New American Chinese food brings that mentality into the base of cooking that I know. It's that same celebration of diversity in the food I taught myself to make and the food that I love.

I'm far from the first person to discuss this idea of third culture, although I wasn't aware of anyone applying the term to food and cooking when I started doing so. When I began posting TikTok videos a couple of years ago that dealt with the topic and how it influenced the way I cooked and thought about food, I noticed that sharing that part of myself really resonated with people. One comment on a video I posted for a pasta dish seasoned with traditional Chinese condiments sticks out in particular: "This felt like watching my Italian mom and Chinese dad conceive me." And while the comment itself was a lesson in how very overfamiliar people are willing to get online, it showed me that many people can relate to this notion of expressing ourselves through food in a way that not only reflects our complicated identities but also affirms them. These were topics I sort of innately understood for myself, but it wasn't until I started getting those kinds of comments on social media that I realized many people wanted a name to assign to those feelings and to legitimize them. If you're gonna be a metaphor, you might as well be a delicious one.

Nostalgia really does so much in shaping our understanding of what good food is and in some sense what our cultural foundations are. When I think of the cuisine I grew up with I think of the crispy pan-fried noodles we ate at the family-owned Chinese restaurant at the local strip mall in Toronto (the one with the arcade game I got to play when I finished my food), or the hearty Hong Kong borscht I ate after school in Hong Kong. There were grilled cheese sandwiches served with canned cream of chicken soup, crispy Shanghainese pork chops, macaroni casserole with flecks of charred broccoli, stir-fried spaghetti with hot dogs and tomatoes, gently steamed green vegetables laced with garlic, Spam-and-egg sandwiches, steak with cream of mushroom sauce and a side of rice, and extra-crunchy chicken wings, marinated in savory fish sauce and white pepper and lightly tossed in baking soda before frying, so the skin crackled when it hit the hot oil and shattered when you bit into it.

These foods might not resemble the expected definition of "Chinese food" to some people. Or what people may eat in a Hong Kong household. And while I might not be able to express all the intricacies of my identity and culture in words, I can do my best to cook you a dish that captures my story—and it's just as much cream of chicken soup with grilled cheese as it is congee.

As long as I've been cooking professionally, I've been on a path to deepen my relationship with Chinese food. Not only to learn more about certain techniques and methods but also to really expand the notions of what it can be. The food I make at my pop-ups and on new media (and now with this book, traditional media . . . la-di-da, look at me) evokes nostalgia, inspires me, and allows me to reconnect with ingredients I grew up with but never fully appreciated. And for all I have learned about Chinese cookery, I will always feel like a student. The cuisine is so immensely vast and varied that there's always more to learn. China might be a single country, but saying you want to master Chinese cuisine is closer to saying you want to master European cuisine rather than that of one of the countries in Europe. I used food as a means to explore my own identity, only to realize that there was more to it than I initially thought. Therapy would have been a more efficient way of going about this, but therapy doesn't come with fries.

One important thing to keep in mind: Chinese cooking is not a monolith. The dishes I grew up with and the way I prepare them are going to be very different from the dishes and cooking styles familiar to other Chinese people, especially since a lot of the time I'm just cooking with nothing more than my childhood memory to guide me. This is the only time you're going to hear this kind of disclaimer from me—I'm not trying to be authentic to anyone but myself here.

Here ends the disclaimer that every POC cookbook author has to write because culturally insecure people on the Internet love to call to question their authenticity just because we don't cook exactly the same way they do, or their grandma did.

When you consider how broad the Chinese food experience can be, you start to see that the techniques of Chinese cooking are a good lens through which to look at other cultures, and finding connections and illustrating similarities in cultural foods are what I love doing. Once you free yourself from the strict dogma of "traditional cuisine," you'll become excited by new recipes instead of being intimidated by trying to perfect them, and you'll find inspiration in unexpected places.

One example is an American Chinese dish that's beloved here in Michigan, where I live now: almond boneless chicken. It's battered and fried chicken cut into thick slices, laid over a bed of iceberg lettuce, and topped with a mild brown gravy, toasted almonds, and a sprinkling of scallions. It's a local icon, and despite being very old-school, some newer restaurants will take a stab at their own interpretations of it.

While no one can pinpoint exactly where the dish originated, the fact that on older menus it's sometimes called war su gai—a Cantonese name that means roughly "wok-seared chicken"—might offer a clue. It's likely that the dish has its roots in Taishan, a region of Southeast China where many of the first Chinese Americans came from, and that, over time, it was adapted to white American tastes (the chicken deep-fried rather than stir-fried and the toasted almonds added).

Almond boneless chicken evolved in a similar way to other American Chinese dishes such as chow mein and orange chicken and, more broadly, Chinese immigrant cooking around the world: Take a traditional Chinese dish, adapt it with new ingredients for new tastes, and sell it to non-Chinese consumers. Every wave of Chinese immigrants brought their own regional influences, resulting in dishes such as kung pao chicken from Szechuan and General Tso's from Taiwan. The most familiar examples are staples like beef and broccoli, cashew chicken, sweet-and-sour pork, and crab rangoon. But this Chinese culinary inventiveness wasn't limited to the United States. It's in Peru. India. Australia. Each immigrant community invented new takes on traditional Chinese dishes that reflected their third-culture experience—taking a beloved dish from home and re-creating it based on available ingredients. It could be something as simple as fried rice made with Mexican chorizo or a stuffed scallion pancake seasoned with Malaysian curry spices. It's food that's not limited by physical borders or meaningless rules of authenticity. It's resource-ful, it's inventive, and it's in line with the way so many Americans cook in our homes now.

So why is "fusion" a dirty word in culinary circles? In the early 1980s, Wolfgang Puck started fusing Asian flavors with French and Californian cuisines at his LA restaurant Chinois on Main, and while his trailblazing work was thoughtful, creative, and playful, soon every nightclub with a kitchen hopped on the fusion train and smothered everything from wings to pizza rolls in teriyaki sauce and spicy mayo. The result, thirty-plus years later, is that *nobody* wants their food labeled "fusion"—which is funny, because that's what most American chefs cook, myself included. At the end of the day, my cooking *is* a kind of fusion. And if I admit it, if we all admit it, maybe we can make it less of a dirty word than it used to be.

This new fusion that I'm referring to as "third culture" takes a more thoughtful approach to the genre. It was so apparent back when it was an eighties fad that it mostly comprised Western chefs slapping on an "exotic" ingredient without any real care for whether it worked. It was a one-sided exercise really meant to be enjoyed by one com-munity. Third culture embraces each side as equal, drawing from a lived experience that is immersed in both or multiple cultures, once again taking the mentality of the American culinary renaissance that came around in the 2010s and granting the rest of us the ability to take part in it. Because what was that food anyway but white American chefs realizing they could take part in the diversity of the communities around them? What's stopping us from doing the same?

My interest in third-culture cooking has taught me that the only things any of us can claim are our own stories, our own experiences, and our own memories. Food and culture are constantly changing, and if we embrace that concept, we can keep the traditions we do have—both old and new—close to our hearts. We're learning from the past and, hopefully, crafting something new and delicious to feed ourselves and those we care most about right now, in our present.

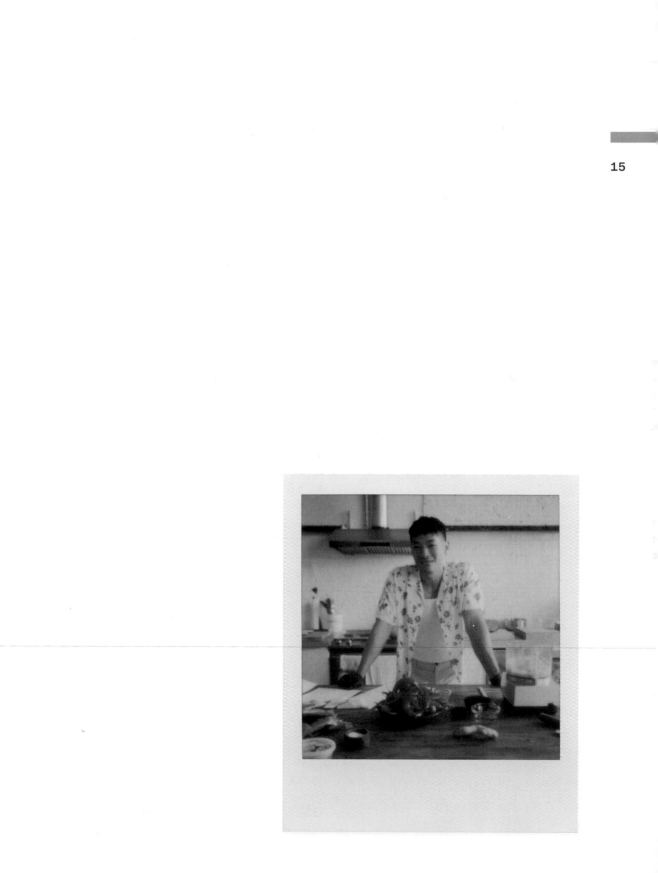

Introduction

Power to the Pantry

A good pantry smells like the world.

The power of the American pantry comes from its diversity: Where some might keep ketchup on the shelf, I always have olive vegetable, a Chinese salt-preserved olive and mustard green paste that's kind of like our answer to olive tapenade (I love adding it to congee and using it as a ready-made topping for rice and noodles). It sits next to a jar of ghee, a massive tub of tahini, and some Nigerian palm oil, among dozens, if not hundreds, of other little jars, bags, and containers from all around the world. There are so many exciting ingredients available to us, and shopping online makes most of what is sold in big cities accessible to people in more rural areas (and time-crunched people in big cities). This gives us an opportunity to learn from and support one another, as well as to create dishes that are unique to us as people of distant cultures who are now neighbors. To me, that is the best part of American home cooking.

The ingredients and equipment on the pages that follow are common to Chinese diasporic cooking and are essential for making the recipes in this book. Almost all these ingredients have extremely long shelf lives, so one shopping trip will set you up for a while.

Ingredients

Soy Sauces

Soy sauces vary by country, and even within specific regions of those countries. While some sources say that Japanese and Chinese soy sauces can be used interchangeably, I don't find that to be the case. **Japanese shoyu** (or tamari, if you have a wheat sensitivity) tends to be less salty and lighter-bodied than **Chinese soy sauce**. I would rather stock my pantry with smaller bottles of various soy sauces (which store very well at room temperature due to their salt content) than one large bottle to use in an all-purpose way.

LIGHT SOY SAUCE

There are two primary categories of soy sauce that you need to know and that I refer to often in my recipes: light and dark. **Light soy sauce** is what most cooks know as "soy sauce"; it has a thin texture and high salt content. (People sometimes ask me why I don't add salt to some of my dishes, and the reason is that soy sauce *is* the salt.) The word "light" here has to do with consistency, not calories or sodium content. I don't bother with low-sodium soy sauces; I'd rather just use less soy sauce. Most low-sodium soy sauces contain about 40 percent of the sodium of the original, so if you're watching your salt intake, simply cut the soy sauce quantity in the recipe in half.

DARK SOY SAUCE

Dark soy sauce has a deeper color and thicker, more viscous consistency, and it's used more as an ingredient than a condiment (although a couple drops of dark soy sauce is a nice way to top a sunny-side-up egg over rice). In a braising liquid, it adds complexity of flavor as well as color—most "red-braised" or "red-cooked" dishes rely on dark soy sauce as a key ingredient. A third product, popular in Indonesia, is sweet soy sauce or kecap manis; this is dark soy sauce with a lot of sugar, and usually spices, added.

Good Chinese brands of light and dark soy sauces that are widely available in North America include Lee Kum Kee and Pearl River Bridge; Japanese soy sauce brands I like include Yamasa and Kishibori. In this book, when I call for soy sauce, it's a Chinese brand by default; just remember that Chinese and Japanese soy sauces aren't interchangeable.

Vinegars

Chinese vinegars tend to be milder than their Western counterparts and are used both as an ingredient and a condiment.

WHITE RICE VINEGAR

White rice vinegar (sometimes labeled as rice wine vinegar, which is the same thing—and which is totally different from rice wine, which is not a vinegar) is most often used for cooking, to add simple acidity, as in the Szechuan stir-fried potatoes on page 208.

ZHENJIANG BLACK VINEGAR

Zhenjiang (or **Chinkiang**) **black vinegar** is made from black rice but can sometimes include wheat in its production process, so check the ingredient list if you can't eat gluten. It's acidic but not overpowering, and has a malty, sweet finish. This complexity makes it popular as a dipping sauce for dumplings and as a base for dressings for cold dishes like wood ear mushrooms.

RED VINEGAR

Red vinegar is a specialized vinegar made with red yeast rice. It's less acidic than white rice vinegar and is often used as a condiment with seafood. True red vinegar can be hard to find in the US; most bottles I see are diluted white vinegar with added food coloring. If you find a bottle of true red vinegar, buy it. It's a good thing to add to your condiment lineup for noodle bowls, soup dumplings, and the like.

Shaoxing Wine

In most Chinese households you'll find a bottle of this amber-colored **cooking wine**, which is used as a deglazing liquid to add aromatic richness to stir-fries as well as to counterbalance gamy and fishy flavors. Dry sherry is sometimes used as a substitute, but since sherry is usually more expensive than Shaoxing wine, and has quite a different flavor, it's not a perfect swap. Because of American laws and licensing restrictions, most Shaoxing wines have salt added (so they can be sold as "cooking wine" on supermarket shelves instead of restricted to liquor stores), and that's the wine I use in the recipes in this book. If you're able to find Shaoxing wine with no salt added, by all means, use it and just add salt to the dish if necessary.

If you avoid alcohol, try making a very concentrated miso stock with certified halal miso (guaranteed to be free of alcohol, which is sometimes used in miso as an additive) to use in place of Shaoxing wine. Dissolve 2 tablespoons miso paste per 1 cup boiling water. It doesn't taste like Shaoxing wine, but the saltiness and fermented aromas of the miso make for a decent nonalcoholic substitute.

Miso

Miso is a Japanese paste made of fermented soybeans and a rice culture called koji. The most common varieties of miso are **shiro**, **shinshu**, and **aka** (white, yellow, and red, respectively), with shiro being the mildest and aka the strongest. Simply dissolving miso paste in water (1 tablespoon miso to about 1¼ cups water) is my favorite way to make a quick broth.

Cooking Fats

NEUTRAL OIL

Peanut oil is my preferred cooking oil. It has a high smoke point of 450°F and a mild enough flavor and aroma (hence the term "neutral oil") that it takes well to stir-fries, deep-fried foods, and flavored oils. Refined peanut oil used for cooking is safe for those with peanut allergies, since it's the peanut proteins (which are filtered out), not the fat (which is what peanut oil is), that trigger allergic reactions. The FDA doesn't require highly refined oils to include food allergy labeling for this reason. Almost all the peanut oil sold in supermarkets (especially in large containers) is refined, even though it's not labeled as such. Unrefined peanut oil has a strong peanut flavor and is usually labeled as "unrefined," "cold-pressed," "expeller-pressed," or "expressed."

Other neutral oils with a high smoke point (since the oil is heated when making flavored oils, include **refined avocado oil** (520°F smoke point) and **grapeseed oil** (390°F), two of my favorites, but **soybean oil** (450°F), **tea seed oil** (486°F), **sunflower oil** (450°F), and **corn oil** (450°F) are acceptable as well.

GHEE

Ghee is a type of clarified butter that is widely used in South Asian and Desi cooking. While it's rarely used in traditional Chinese food, I—a curry lover—find it to be a kitchen necessity. It has all the flavor of butter with the addition of a high smoke point (450°F). It adds richness to pan-fried dishes and releases the aromas of spices gorgeously. Because the milk solids have been cooked out and removed, ghee can be stored at room temperature and has a very long shelf life. That said, it should be used within six months of opening.

OLIVE OIL

The strong flavor of **olive oil** tends to clash in Chinese dishes, but it still has a place in mixed-culture cooking. I use it mostly for salad dressings and when roasting meats and vegetables in the oven.

The Foundational Trio

Garlic, ginger, and scallions form a kind of holy trinity of aromatics whose role in Cantonese cooking is indispensable.

GARLIC

Garlic is native to Central Asia, and today China produces the vast majority of the world's supply. Most supermarket garlic is softneck garlic, as opposed to hardneck garlic, which has a rigid central flower stalk. Hardneck garlic tends to have a stronger flavor than softneck and is worth looking for in farmers' markets. I prefer to grate my garlic cloves with a Microplane or other fine grater, but feel free to mince if that's easier for you.

GINGER

Ginger can take the "fishiness" off seafood, infuse warmth and brightness to savory dishes, and add a punchy heat to sweets. I find that Western supermarkets and chain grocery stores prefer to stock younger gingerroots, which are smaller, with many nubby "fingers." They're more visually appealing, but they're a pain in the butt to peel and milder in flavor. Larger, older roots are drier and more fibrous but also tend to have more flavor and heat. Older ginger is easy to find in most Asian grocery stores. There's a Chinese saying: "The older the ginger, the spicier it gets"—meaning that with age comes wisdom.

SCALLIONS

Scallions are more than just the world's most functional garnish. They impart an oniony note in a way that isn't overpowering, whereas regular onions would be too pungent. While they usually play a supporting role in many dishes, scallions are the star of Ginger Scallion Oil (page 53), one of my favorite Chinese condiments.

Starches

Besides **cornstarch** and wheat flour (i.e., all-purpose flour), I always have potato starch and tapioca flour on hand. **Tapioca flour** has a neutral flavor, helps baked goods (like waffles) become golden brown and crispy, and adds a glossy sheen to sauces. **Potato starch** (which is different from potato flour) works much like cornstarch to thicken sauces and give a crispy coating to deep-fried foods, with the bonus of having a pleasantly mild flavor and an ability to withstand long cooking at high heat. Both are inexpensive and worth buying for any recipes here that call for them.

Salt

Different kinds of salt—kosher, sea, table—vary in intensity, and even varying brands of the same type of salt will give different outcomes. Also, the density of salt in a standard measure (such as a teaspoon) varies depending on how finely or coarsely it's ground. For the sake of clarity, when I say "salt," I'm specifically using Diamond Crystal kosher salt. If you're using another type of salt, start with half the quantity and adjust from there by taste.

MSG

Monosodium glutamate is the combination of glutamic acid (naturally found in our bodies as well as in most things we find delicious, such as mushrooms, tomatoes, cheese, and meat) combined with sodium (salt). Because of this combination it adds a well-rounded fullness of flavor we describe as savory or umami (in Chinese we call it xian wei). Like salt, when used correctly it makes food taste like a better version of itself, and also like salt, if you use too much that can be all you taste. Use it sparingly, in quantities like a quarter to an eighth of the amount of salt you'd add in a recipe.

Spices

Spices provide nuance to a dish and comprise at least three-quarters of my personality. They add layers of aroma to the base tastes of sweet, bitter, sour, salt, and umami and act as bridges that connect those flavors in a harmonious way. Think of these five base tastes as primary colors, and herbs and spices as the infinite "in-between" that turns them into a rainbow.

BAY LEAF

I know people joke that bay leaves don't smell or taste like anything, but if that's the case with yours, it just means they're old and need to be replaced. An herb in spice drag, bay leaf adds earthiness and astringency to dishes, with a smell that recalls eucalyptus, sage, and pine. It's a good grounding note in acidic or pungent dishes like meaty stews or tomato sauces, which benefit from steeping the leaves in their liquid.

CARDAMOM (GREEN)

One of the most expensive spices by weight, the green cardamom pod imparts an intense and unique aroma to any food. Bright, citrusy, floral, and cooling, it also has a spicy herbal note that reminds me of eucalyptus. To me, it has the aroma of vitality and alertness. Essential

in Indian cuisine, it's used in a variety of sweets and in coffee, too. A few drops of cardamom bitters in some sparkling water tastes like a classic cream soda without the sugar.

CARDAMOM (BLACK)

Black cardamom is in the same family as green cardamom but is a different genus and species. It has similar tones to green cardamom, but because of the way it's dried over an open flame, it takes on an intensely smoky and somewhat medicinal aroma. It has a strong presence in Szechuan cuisine, and it still contains the cooling mentholated qualities of its green cousin but to a lesser extent: Think smoke and snowflakes from a campfire at night with pine needles overhead. To use green or black cardamom, depending on the recipe, the pod can be gently crushed in your fingers or used whole, or the seeds can be removed from the pod and added to spice blends.

CINNAMON

While it's associated with sweets in Western cuisine, cinnamon is used in other countries to balance savory dishes. It's every bit at home adding its warmth to roast lamb or pork, soy sauce braises, and spice blends as it is in a sticky bun. Cinnamon's versatility shines when you realize that its aroma isn't sweet, per se, but warm—and you can add warmth to just about anything.

CLOVES

Cloves are dried flower buds with an intensely sweet and spicy flavor, almost like a cross between cinnamon and vanilla. Common to Asia, Africa, the Caribbean, and the Middle East, the clove brings depth to curries, stews, and marinades. It's also used as a foundational low note with ingredients like pears, citrus, pumpkin, rhubarb, and apples. In the US, we see it in the colder months in fruit and mincemeat pies, spiced cakes, mulled wines, and hot ciders and for studding oranges and hams. In Chinese cuisine, it's mostly used in savory dishes and as a component of Five-Spice Powder (page 59).

CORIANDER SEED

Raw, the smell of coriander seed isn't very distinct, but when heated, its aromas are lemony and floral, and to me it smells like Froot Loops. Though this might make it seem ideal for sweet applications, coriander is more often found in savory dishes such as curries and pickle brines, and as a component of dried meats and sausages. It was also one of the original ingredients in Coca-Cola.

CUMIN

Most people are familiar with cumin's use in Mexican and South Asian cuisine, but it's also common in Chinese cooking, where it's often paired with ginger and white pepper. It has an earthy scent with notes of wood and even musk, and when it's toasted before use, a bright citrus note comes out. It's a great counterbalance to stronger-flavored meats like lamb, goat, duck, or game.

DRIED CHILIES

Szechuan chilies can be found in large bags in Chinese grocery stores, labeled simply as "chili pepper." They most likely come from the zhi tian jiao or seven star chili pepper plant. Comparable with Thai chilies at around 60,000 Scoville heat units (SHU), they're far from the world's spiciest peppers (Scotch bonnets go up to 350,000 SHU, and Carolina Reapers can surpass 2 million SHU), but they well exceed, for example, the heat of a jalapeño, which at its spiciest may reach only 8,000 SHU. Any dried hot red chilies, such as chiles de árbol, can be substituted for Szechuan chilies.

DRIED MUSHROOMS

Mushrooms are a huge flavor resource when making stocks or sauces. Dried mushrooms are even more concentrated, and it can be useful to think of them as a spice. I almost always include mushrooms in my broths, regardless of whether the reconstituted mushroom ends up in the final product. Some mushrooms contribute specific flavors, and others add more of a background depth and body to a broth. Hua gu mushrooms (a high grade of shiitake, sold whole) and wood ears (a gelatinous mushroom that comes in off-black and off-white colors) are rehydrated and often consumed on their own as a side dish.

Along with chicken bouillon powder, mushroom bouillon powder is a major source of full umami in my soups and dishes. Available in any Asian grocery, this powdered form is easy to measure and mix into a variety of things. I like the Lee Kum Kee brand, but I also look for larger bags from brands without any English on the label, since they tend to be cheaper.

FENNEL SEED

Fennel seed is actually not a seed, but the dried fruit of the plant, which contains even smaller seeds within. It's an essential element in both Chinese Five-Spice Powder (page 59) and Indian garam masala. Like aniseed, it makes food seem sweeter without added sugar. It's also recognized throughout Asia as a digestive aid. Look for dried fennel seeds that are still bright green. The seeds gray over time, indicating a loss of potency, which just means you may want to use a little more of it.

JUJUBES

Jujubes, or Chinese dates, are far less sweet than Medjool dates or other varieties you may be familiar with, which are essentially pure sugar. Jujubes have a citrusy finish that gives them complexity. They're often stewed in syrup as a dessert, but I like adding them to savory soups and broths to give a hint of sweetness for balance.

PEPPER (BLACK)

Black pepper is the most popular household seasoning in the US next to salt, but still manages to be one of the most underestimated. Its versatility is astounding, giving off different aromatic characteristics and qualities depending on whether it's toasted or raw, and cracked, crushed, or ground. I love the bright fragrance of the Tellicherry variety and how well it stands up to roasting. Always start with whole peppercorns, and crush or grind them just before using. Store peppercorns that aren't in your pepper mill in an airtight jar in a cool, dark place.

PEPPER (WHITE)

White pepper and black pepper come from the same plant. Black pepper is a dried whole unripe fruit of that plant; the peppercorns are picked when they're still green, but an enzyme in their skin turns it black as they dry in the sun. White pepper comes from that same fruit, but it is allowed to fully mature before harvest. The flesh of the fruit ferments and is then removed, and the seed within becomes what we know as a white peppercorn. It has a subtle flavor, losing some of the sharpness and heat of black pepper but with a delicious herbal quality, made more complex if it's toasted before being ground. White pepper loses its flavor much faster than black pepper does, so it's even more important to use whole peppercorns instead of pre-ground pepper. Many of my recipes include both black pepper and white pepper, and I implore you to resist the urge to use black pepper only; it's no more complicated to use both than simply pulling one more jar from the spice cabinet.

SAND GINGER (AND OTHER GALANGALS)

Four very different rhizomes are labeled and sold as "galangal" in fresh, dried, and powdered forms. While all are in the ginger family, they play very different culinary roles. The one I use most is known as dried sand ginger (and that's how I've called for it in the book). Sand ginger is widely used in Chinese medicine as well as in Chinese cuisine, where it's frequently paired with chicken. It adds a gently astringent, even medicinal quality to foods, with a taste that can be described as peppery, citrusy, and piney. The other galangal you're likely to see is usually labeled "greater galangal," and it is used fresh in Southeast Asian cooking. It has more of a mentholated flavor than sand ginger. I don't recommend substituting one type of galangal for another.

SESAME SEEDS

Sesame seeds add nuttiness to savory dishes as well as sweets. Their flavor is accentuated by toasting in a dry skillet, but take care when doing so, as they burn quickly. Toast them by placing in a dry pan over medium heat, stirring continuously, until they're aromatic and starting to darken in color. If you're cooking them along with other ingredients in a dish, leave them untoasted so they don't burn. When I call for sesame seeds, they're always hulled, because unhulled ones can be bitter and overly hard in texture. Most Asian groceries sell both raw and toasted sesame seeds, allowing you to skip the toasting process yourself. Because of their oil content sesame seeds can go rancid rather quickly. They will smell a little bit like old oil when they do.

STAR ANISE

A key ingredient of five-spice powder, star anise adds a sweet aroma that goes well with most meats, but especially with beef, pork, and chicken. While some people are put off by the licorice flavor of the whole spice, the richness it adds when infused into the savory notes of soy sauce makes it absolutely essential to a Chinese kitchen. The combination of star anise and cooked onion can mimic flavors of cooked beef; it accentuates meat dishes and adds a meatlike quality to vegetarian dishes like stir-fried tofu and braised mushrooms.

SZECHUAN PEPPER

Szechuan pepper is a core spice in Szechuan cuisine and, with chili, makes up half the seasoning combination that creates mala (麻辣), a sensation of numbing (麻 ma) and spicy (辣 la) in the mouth. (Despite the name, Szechuan pepper is neither closely related to black and white peppercorns, nor to chili peppers—it's a berry from the prickly ash shrub, a plant related to citrus. There is also a green variety with brighter notes of citrus and a fresher aroma. It also has the numbing effect.) The peppercorns are often steeped in oil, and the oil then imparts the flavor and sensation in the food, which gives the cook more control than using the peppercorns themselves. From 1968 to 2005, Szechuan pepper was banned from being imported into the US because it carried a disease harmful to US citrus crops. However, the ban was not strictly enforced, and many Americans were able to taste it in Szechuan restaurants. Today, it's easy to find.

Equipment

Woks

There are two main wok styles you'll run into, Cantonese and Mandarin. Cantonese woks have two metal loops for handles, one on each side, while Mandarin woks have a long straight handle on one side, much like a regular frying pan. There are also hybrid woks with a large handle on one side and a Cantonese handle on the other.

Which style is the best is a matter of preference. If you're accustomed to Western pans, you might want to consider a Mandarin wok, especially for cooking over an open-flame like a gas range. If you prefer a very large wok, the Cantonese style is probably better.

A Note About Induction

If you're serious about upping your wok game, think about getting an induction burner to use with a cast-iron or carbon-steel wok. Gas and electric cooktops use thermal conduction to heat the burner, which then transfers heat to the pan. Induction cooking uses an electromagnetic process to create heat in the material of the pan itself (provided that material is compatible); the "burner" itself remains cool to the touch. As a result, induction can bring pans to higher temperatures than electric or gas burners, making it perfect for wok cooking (both cast iron and carbon steel are compatible with induction). If you don't have an induction cooktop, you can buy a stand-alone induction burner that plugs into the wall to make a dedicated wok station. I've noticed some newer induction units don't switch off when the pan is lifted, or they will turn back on when the pan has been put back after a short time. Still, if you're going to do that, do it very gently because you run the risk of scratching or breaking the cooktop. I use an induction wok burner that's concave and protected from impact to accommodate round-bottomed woks as well as the stir-frying motion. If you're really serious about stir-fries, investing in one of these is totally worth it.

In terms of materials, don't bother with stainless-steel or nonstick. Stainless-steel woks scorch easily and are hard to clean; they're best for liquid cooking, like steaming or braising. Wok temperatures can and should exceed 650°F, while nonstick coatings are generally rated safe up to only 500°F.

Instead, cast iron is a great, if heavy, option. Western home burners usually don't have the sheer power output needed to maintain the temperatures necessary for real wok cooking, so having a cast-iron wok can help. If you're a beginner to wok cooking and have a flat top stove of any kind, I would suggest a Lodge cast-iron wok. It's Cantonese-style with a flat bottom that is too heavy to allow for any kind of "tossing" motion, but it does a good job retaining the heat needed for wok cooking. This also makes it a good wok for deep-frying.

Carbon steel has similar properties and care requirements to cast iron, with the benefit of being much lighter. It's the preferred material for most professional kitchens and, like cast iron, can be seasoned to a nearly nonstick finish. The lightness is the only downside when compared with cast iron: Because it's so thin, it can easily drop in temperature if the heat source isn't powerful enough. If you don't have a high-BTU-output gas stove with a dedicated wok burner, carbon steel might not be the wok material for you. However, a flat bottom carbon-steel wok on an induction burner is probably the best and safest way to achieve those wok temperatures at home. Still, use caution; I underestimated mine the first time I used it and ignited the oil in my wok.

Read This Before Cooking Anything in a Wok!

If you're serious about wok cooking, you need to preseason your wok before you use it, every time. This ensures you'll have a fresh nonstick surface on the pan each time you cook in it. In all the recipes here that involve a wok, this preseasoning step is assumed and encouraged.

1. Keep a few cups of neutral oil in a heatproof jar or metal-lidded container to use as your precooking seasoning.

2. After you've prepped and pulled out all the ingredients (stir-frying and wok cooking happen quickly, so doing a preliminary read-though is really helpful), heat the wok over high heat until it starts to give off little wisps of white smoke. Add a ladle full of oil to the wok, swirl it around with a ladle, and then carefully return the oil to the jar. The seasoning oil can be reused repeatedly; toss it if and when it begins to smell rancid. You may give the wok a wipe with some paper towels or a clean old rag with tongs to get any excess oil out if there's still a lot there. The point is to achieve a bone-dry surface. Your wok is ready for action.

3. Now add however much *fresh* cooking oil to the wok as the recipe instructs and swirl it around the wok before you begin stir-frying.

4. After you're done cooking, while the wok is still hot, rinse it with water and scrub it with a rough brush (don't use soap, as it will remove the seasoning). We use a brush made of large bamboo sticks to get stuck-on pieces out of the wok. That's about all you need to do to clean the wok, unless things are really gummed up on the surface. Once it's clean and dry, rub the wok with a very thin coating of the seasoning oil before putting it away.

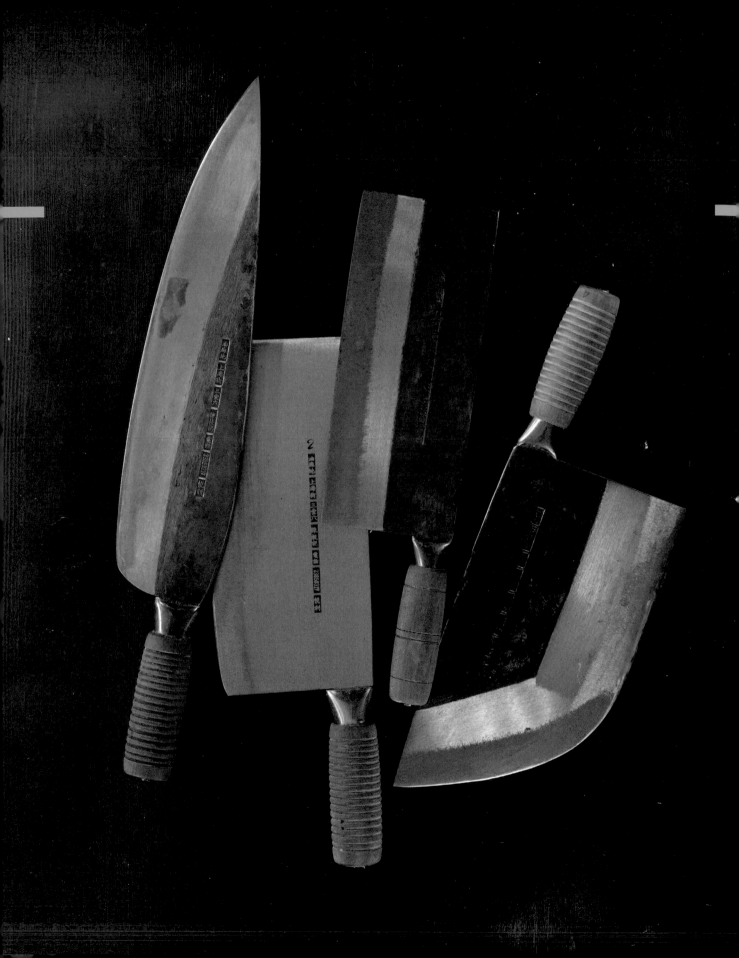

Mortar and Pestle/Spice Grinder

If you're going to cook with whole spices (and you should), you will constantly be grinding them. I recommend having both a large mortar and pestle as well as a good electric spice grinder. A mortar and pestle is best for smaller quantities (the large size is so the spices don't escape as you crush them), large spices like cinnamon sticks, and "wet" items like ginger, lemongrass, and fresh herbs. The electric spice grinder is best for quickly pulverizing larger quantities of dried spices into powder.

The best electric spice grinders have a detachable stainless-steel bowl that can be easily washed by hand or in the dishwasher. Stainless steel is nonporous, so it won't absorb the oils from one batch of ground spices and transfer them to the next.

The Tea/Spice Strainer

If you're going to do a lot of braising, stewing, or poaching with whole spices (as I do), having a large metal tea strainer is indispensable for saving time and your sanity. Spices are great for a broth, but if you're cooking things you want to eat in that broth along with the spices, straining can get pretty messy. They make large strainers—like reusable mesh steel tea balls but larger—that you can put small spices in, add to your pot, and then just remove when you're done. It's like you would with muslin or cheesecloth, but you only have to buy it once.

Knives

When most inexperienced cooks come across a Chinese cleaver, their instinct seems to fall somewhere around the "Hulk smash" region of care and finesse. This is understandable, since the Western use of cleaver-shaped knives is associated with butchers whacking away at animal bones. However, Chinese culinary knives are much more varied than people realize. The thinness of a cleaver-shaped blade can vary greatly depending on its intended use. A small vegetable cleaver, while humble in appearance, can be as sharp as any specialized Japanese knife meant for delicate slicing.

There are other specialty knives used for the butchering process, but two Chinese cleavers I would consider essential are a small vegetable cleaver (to use as a chef's knife alternative) and a bone cleaver (meant for splitting bones but equally effective on hard squashes and melons). Other knives I keep in my kitchen are a Western chef's knife, a serrated bread knife, and a paring knife.

I also consider a mandoline indispensable to my knife arsenal for very thin slicing. It seems to be the kitchen tool that inspires the most fear, and you need only one incident with a mandoline to learn lifelong respect for this outrageously sharp instrument. It's absolutely worth the price for its usefulness—just be careful (or buy a stainless-steel mesh glove to keep your fingers protected when slicing).

Steaming Baskets

If you've been to a dim sum restaurant, you've seen steamer baskets stacked on top of one another, keeping a variety of treasures warm, from steamed buns to soup dumplings to short ribs. Having one or two of these baskets at home opens you up to a healthy way of cooking as well as maximizing the utility of your wok, which acts as a base for the baskets. Bamboo baskets are easiest to find, but metal (and dishwasher-safe) ones are available as well. Steaming baskets are also ideal for gently reheating multiple leftovers at once and cooking a plethora of ready-to-steam dim sum dishes from the frozen foods aisle. They're great for heating frozen tamales, too.

Candy/Deep-Fry Thermometer

A candy thermometer or instant-read digital thermometer is essential for deep-frying or making my chili oils and other oil-based infusions. An instant-read thermometer can also check the temperature of meat to ensure it's cooked to a safe temperature or to your desired degree of doneness before serving.

Rice Cookers

Rice cookers hold a special place in any Asian household. The sheer convenience of having the essential meal component taken care of in a near foolproof one-button process leaves you free to focus on other dishes. Cookers that feature a vacuum seal and a "keep warm" function further stretch the utility of these machines as warming stations, keeping rice, soups, porridge, or congee moist and at a safe temperature for hours at a time.

High-end rice cookers can cook brown rice and other grains, make porridge or congee, or even cook mixed rice dishes for a one-pot meal. Of all the countertop appliances that some might deem "optional," a really nice rice cooker is one I encourage all rice-loving people to invest in. Your life will be better. It will. I promise.

Three professionals and a TikTok guy.

Broths, Condiments, Spice Blends, and an All-Purpose Egg

Cooks that don't measure understand that going slightly (or in certain cases even way) over on some spices doesn't really make a difference. It's going under by any amount that is unforgivable.

Some traditional and some not, these key flavor drivers always have a place in my cupboard and fridge. Many of the recipes in this book refer back to these basics as core ingredients, but they can also transform a simple plate of noodles, rice, cold chicken, or steamed veggies on their own.

Herbal Chicken Broth

Makes about 2 quarts

1 large roaster chicken or
    stewing hen (about 5 pounds)
1½ cups sliced peeled fresh
    ginger (about 6 ounces)
8 scallions, chopped
1 cup dried shiitake mushrooms
2 pieces dried sand ginger,
    cracked in a mortar and
    pestle or using a rolling pin
1 tablespoon chicken bouillon
    powder
2 teaspoons cracked white
    peppercorns
6 jujubes
3 star anise pods
Kosher salt (optional)

This is the perfect base broth for noodle and dumpling soups, any chicken-based dish, and anywhere that "chicken broth" is called for in this book. Stewing hens—older egg-laying chickens—can be hard to come by, but if your butcher has them, they give the richest flavor to chicken broths. You can also often find them frozen at Chinese groceries. You might notice that I bring water and chicken to a boil, discard the water, and then bring it to a simmer again. This does a few things: It gets rid of most of the scummy proteins to ensure a clearer broth, makes a purer-tasting stock, and removes much of the gaminess of the older bird. You're also cooking it at a lower temperature in the second pass; the water shouldn't be a rolling boil, just releasing some tiny bubbles every now and then.

Put the chicken in a large stockpot and add water to cover. Bring to a boil over high heat and cook for about 5 minutes. Some foam and scum will rise to the surface, which is what you're looking for; use a skimmer to discard this now for a clearer stock later. Drain the chicken in a colander and rinse under cold running water. Rinse out the pot and return the chicken to it.

Add the ginger, scallions, mushrooms, sand ginger, bouillon, white pepper, jujubes, and star anise to the pot and cover with cold water. Bring to a boil over high heat, then reduce the heat to low and simmer, uncovered, for at least 2 hours, at which point most of the chicken flavor will have been released into the broth.

Remove the chicken and either discard it or pick the meat to use later or freeze, then strain the stock into a large bowl (discard the solids). Taste and add salt if necessary. Let cool, then transfer to a tightly covered container and store in the refrigerator for up to a week or in the freezer for up to 6 months.

Vegan Broth

Makes about 3 quarts

2 yellow onions, quartered
1 head garlic, cloves separated
    and smashed in their skins
1 cup sliced fresh ginger
8 scallions, chopped
2 plum tomatoes, quartered
1 cup dried porcini mushrooms
1 cup dried shiitake mushrooms
1 cup store-bought roasted
    barley or Korean barley tea
1 tablespoon cracked black
    peppercorns
8 jujubes
5 star anise pods
1 cinnamon stick
2 black cardamom pods,
    cracked
1 teaspoon MSG
2 teaspoons light soy sauce
Kosher salt
1 tablespoon miso paste
    (optional)

When coming up with a vegan broth, I wanted something that would match the umami, and also the richness, of a meat-based broth. That's why mushrooms and roasted barley really shine here: Together, they add both depth of flavor and body, creating a base onto which you build with brighter and bolder aromatics. MSG should find its way into most vegan broths because it's so much more efficient at adding flavor than salt is (it's added to most bouillons and soup powders, including the chicken bouillon in the Herbal Chicken Broth, see opposite page).

Preheat the oven to 450°F. Line a baking sheet with parchment paper.

Place the onions, garlic, ginger, scallions, and tomatoes on the lined baking sheet and roast for about 30 minutes, until the scallions have charred and the onions have some color. Transfer the contents of the baking sheet to a stockpot and add the porcini, shiitakes, barley, pepper, jujubes, star anise, cinnamon, cardamom, MSG, soy sauce, 1 tablespoon salt, and miso paste (if using). Add 1 gallon (16 cups) water and bring to a boil over high heat. Reduce the heat to low and simmer, uncovered, for 1 hour.

At this point, taste the broth: If it's too concentrated, you can add more water. If it's not flavorful enough, simmer longer to continue to reduce it. Strain into a large bowl (discard the solids) and add salt to taste. Let cool, then transfer to a tightly covered container and store in the refrigerator for up to a week or in the freezer for up to 6 months.

Superior Stock

Makes about 3 quarts

1 cup sliced fresh ginger
8 scallions, chopped
1 large roaster chicken or
    stewing hen (about 5 pounds)
1 pound pork neck bones
8 ounces Chinese cured ham or
    ham hocks
1 tablespoon cracked white
    peppercorns
¼ cup dried shrimp or scallops
    (optional)
Kosher salt

As you can see from the ingredient list, this is an incredibly flavorful stock, and as its name tells you, it is the best possible stock for any recipe in this book that asks for stock. Why? Think of this as a bottle of "the good stuff," and use it like you would use premium cheeses for your mac and cheese or a can of good tomatoes from Italy when making pomodoro sauce. It transforms anything from braised vegetables, to stewed meatballs (see page 111), to oxtail stew or my "Chinese" feijoada (see page 262). A version of this stock is the signature of every master Cantonese chef. See opposite page for Instant Pot/pressure cooker instructions.

Preheat the oven to 450°F. Line a baking sheet with parchment paper.

Place the ginger and scallions on the lined baking sheet and roast for about 30 minutes, until the scallions start to char.

Meanwhile, put the chicken and pork bones in a large stockpot and cover completely with water. Bring to a boil over high heat and cook for 5 minutes. Drain in a colander, then rinse the chicken and pork bones under cold running water. Rinse out the pot and return the chicken and pork bones to it.

Add the ginger and scallions, the ham, and the white pepper to the pot and cover everything completely with cold water. Bring to a boil over high heat, then reduce the heat to low, cover, and simmer for at least 5 hours, at which point all the flavor will have been extracted from the ingredients. In the last 30 minutes of simmering, add the dried shrimp (if using).

At this point, taste the stock: If it's too strong, add more water. If it's too mild, continue to simmer to reduce it further. Season with salt to taste, then strain the stock into a large bowl (discard the solids). Let cool, then transfer to a tightly covered container and store in the refrigerator for up to a week or in the freezer for up to 6 months.

Automatic Pressure Cooker Superior Stock

Instead of watching over a simmering pot for 5 hours, you can cook the stock using an Instant Pot or electric pressure cooker for 2 hours. (Incorporating the dried seafood, if you're using it, in the last 30 minutes of cooking will still have to be done manually on the stove; otherwise, the stock will be much too fishy.) This method is great not only because it's faster but also because it extracts more gelatin from the bones than the traditional method and leaves you free to leave the house and go about your day without worrying about the stove being on. I pretty much only make my Superior Stock this way now.

Combine all the ingredients in the Instant Pot and seal the lid. Cook on high pressure for 2 hours, then allow the pressure to release naturally. Transfer the stock to a pot on the stove and add the dried shrimp, then bring to a boil over high heat. Reduce the heat to maintain a simmer and cook for 30 minutes, then strain and cool the stock. Use and store as you would the regular superior stock.

The magic of these things isn't just that they reduce the cooking time, it's that they allow you to safely leave the house while they work.

Master Stock

Makes about 8 cups

4 (3-inch) pieces fresh ginger
    (about 6 ounces), unpeeled,
    sliced ¼ inch thick
8 scallions, halved crosswise
1½ tablespoons neutral oil
3 cups store-bought chicken
    broth or mushroom broth
2 cups Shaoxing wine
2 cups light soy sauce
1 cup dark soy sauce
15 star anise pods
5 dried Chinese licorice root
    slivers (see Note, page 43)
5 cinnamon sticks
1½ tablespoons fennel seeds
6 dried sand ginger slices (about
    ¼ inch thick), unpeeled
3 black cardamom pods,
    cracked
1 tablespoon whole cloves
¾ cup rock sugar (or ¼ cup
    lightly packed light brown
    sugar)
1 (3- to 4-pound) whole chicken
1 large Vidalia or other sweet
    onion, sliced

Master stock isn't a "stock," per se, but a braising liquid meant for cooking and poaching meats and mushrooms that can also be used sparingly as a sauce over rice (delicious). It's not meant to be sipped on its own or used as a base for soups. The idea is to use it over and over again—and to keep refreshing it with various ingredients every time so it becomes more flavorful and nuanced as the years go by, almost like how a sourdough mother gets better as it ages because it becomes more complex. It's very ingredient-heavy in the beginning, but it's meant to be reused for years, if taken care of properly, meaning storing it in a tightly covered container in the freezer for up to 6 months between uses. After defrosting, be sure to boil it before using—then cool and refreeze it for another six months, making a master stock that, in theory, you can pass on for generations. This is wonderful for cooking meats like lamb, squab, quail, duck, chicken, beef, and pork, but avoid using it to cook fish, as the oils from the fish will permanently add a pungency to the stock that you don't want in all your other food.

Preheat the broiler and place the broiler rack 4 to 5 inches from the heat source. Line a rimmed baking sheet with aluminum foil.

Toss the ginger, scallions, and oil on the lined baking sheet until coated. Spread them into an even layer and broil until lightly charred, about 3 minutes. Remove from the oven.

Pour the broth, wine, light soy sauce, and dark soy sauce into a large saucepan or stockpot and, tied in some cheesecloth or combined in a tea strainer, add the star anise, licorice root, cinnamon, fennel, sand ginger, cardamom, and cloves. Finally, add the sugar. Bring to a boil over medium-high heat, stirring to dissolve the sugar. Reduce the heat to low and simmer, stirring occasionally, for 1 hour to extract flavor from the spices.

Add the chicken and onion and braise over medium-low heat until the chicken is cooked through, about 45 minutes (check it with a knife at its thickest point to ensure there's no pink meat near the bone).

Remove the chicken from the pot and eat it with rice as a chef's treat. Pour the stock through a fine-mesh strainer into a large heatproof bowl. Let cool for 1 hour, then skim and discard the fat from the surface, if desired. Transfer to an airtight container and store in the refrigerator for up to 1 week or in the freezer for up to 6 months. Before using the master stock each time, thaw it in the fridge, skim the fat, and bring it to a boil; after using, strain, cool, and freeze again for future use.

Note: *Chinese licorice adds a woody sweetness to dishes without the need for additional sugar. Its anise flavor sometimes gets a bad rap, which is too bad because it does such a good job in balancing out savory flavors. It's one of my favorite flavors in the kitchen. You can find it sold in dried slivers.*

Take care of your master stock and it could one day be a family heirloom. Of course they said the same thing about the sourdough starter you made during quarantine ... how's that going?

Basic Chili Oil

Makes about 1 cup

½ cup Szechuan chili flakes
1 cup neutral oil

A basic chili oil is just that: something simple and easy enough to make that can be used as an everyday ingredient and to add kick to any dish. Yes, you can easily buy chili oil, but this recipe couldn't be simpler, and it will hopefully lead you to make the Fragrant Chili Oil (see opposite page), which is better than anything you'll find in a store. All you need are two things: chili flakes (specifically made from Szechuan chilies for their aroma and heat) and neutral oil. This is the chili oil you would use for any dish that calls for a little heat but isn't relying on the chili as a dominant flavor. Note that this is an oil used strictly for flavoring; do not use this as a cooking oil.

Place the chili flakes in a large metal bowl that will be big enough to contain the bubbling-hot oil when it's poured in.

In a small saucepan, heat the oil over medium-high heat to 300°F. Slowly pour the oil over the chili flakes; it will bubble aggressively as you add it and should smell toasty and warm. Let steep for at least 45 minutes, or until cool to the touch, then strain the oil through a fine-mesh strainer into another metal or glass bowl or a lidded jar. Store at room temperature for up to 1 month or in the fridge for up to 6 months.

Fragrant Chili Oil

Makes about 2 cups

1 cup Szechuan chili flakes
3 tablespoons untoasted hulled sesame seeds
3 tablespoons Szechuan peppercorns
3 tablespoons cracked black peppercorns
6 star anise pods
6 whole cloves
3 large cinnamon sticks
2 black cardamom pods, cracked
2 tablespoons fennel seeds
2 tablespoons coriander seeds
2 cups neutral oil

This is the condiment that sponsors the majority of my happiness. While the Basic Chili Oil (see opposite page) is something you can whip up quickly to add heat to a dish that's already flavorful, this chili oil adds heat plus complex spice notes as well. Think of it this way: Basic chili oil is an ingredient used as part of a greater dish (like Mapo Tofu Curry, page 106), while fragrant chili oil is used as a finisher or a condiment (like in my ten-second dumpling sauce; see page 146). I also put it on noodles, pizza, fried chicken, mac and cheese—really anything I want to elevate with heat, fragrance, and additional spicy flavor (almost everything).

Place the chili flakes, sesame seeds, and Szechuan peppercorns in a large metal bowl that will be big enough to contain the bubbling-hot oil when it's poured in. In a small bowl, combine the black pepper, star anise, cloves, cinnamon, and cardamom. In another small bowl, combine the fennel and coriander.

In a large saucepan, heat the oil over medium-high heat to 300°F. Add the star anise mixture and reduce the heat to lower the oil temperature to 250°F. Add the fennel and coriander seeds and let steep for 45 minutes, checking the temperature often and adjusting the heat, if necessary, to maintain a temperature of roughly 250°F. (At that temperature, the fennel and coriander seeds shouldn't start to burn, but if they do, reduce the heat a little further.)

Strain the oil into an empty bowl (discard the solids), then pour it back into the pot. Heat the oil over medium-high heat to 275°F, then pour it over the chili flake mixture. Let cool, then pour the oil (along with the chili flake mixture) into a jar or other airtight container and store at room temperature for up to 1 month or in the fridge for up to 6 months.

Basic Szechuan Peppercorn Oil

Makes about 1 cup

½ cup Szechuan peppercorns
1 cup neutral oil

Szechuan peppercorn oil is a good way to gradually add the numbing sensation of Szechuan pepper to a dish. It grants you greater control over how much of this sensation you want to add than if you were using the whole spice. The pepper's numbing effect can balance very spicy food, creating the mouthfeel known as mala (麻辣). Because a spicy or numbing sensation is felt rather than tasted, it gives a jarring (at first) feeling of a buzz or a vibration on your tongue, which, in my opinion, is electric. This is a finishing oil as opposed to a cooking oil. I like it as a final garnish on chicken salads, noodle dishes, and rice bowls.

In a small nonstick skillet or wok, toast the peppercorns over low heat until you start to smell their musky citrus notes, about 3 minutes. Immediately transfer them to a quarter sheet pan or plate to stop the cooking process and ensure they don't burn; let cool.

Transfer the peppercorns to a mortar and pound them a few times with the pestle just to crack them, then transfer to a large metal bowl. (If you don't have a mortar and pestle, put them in a zip-top bag and pound with a rolling pin or heavy skillet.)

In a small saucepan, heat the oil over medium-high heat to 300°F. Slowly pour the hot oil over the peppercorns—the oil will bubble more aggressively as it falls into the bowl. Set aside to cool completely, then strain through a fine-mesh sieve into a jar or other airtight container and store at room temperature for up to 1 month or in the fridge for up to 6 months.

Chorizo Chili Oil

Makes about 2 cups

8 ounces fresh Mexican pork
    chorizo (casings removed,
    if using links)
2 cups Basic Chili Oil (page 44)
½ large shallot, sliced crosswise
2 cinnamon sticks
2 star anise pods
2 whole cloves

In this simple recipe, chorizo cooks confit-style in chili oil until its fat renders out, giving the finished oil a smoky, spicy aroma. It's a two-in-one recipe, since in addition to the oil, you get the added bonus of the confit chorizo bits, which—while admittedly a bit greasy—are a delicious topping for Dan Dan Noodles (page 141), a bowl of rice topped with a fried egg, or even some home fries you made for brunch. Store the oil and fried chorizo bits separately, as their shelf lives differ greatly (obviously, the meat needs to get used up more quickly than the oil). Mexican chorizo is a soft fresh sausage, as opposed to Spanish chorizo, which is firm and cured. If you can't find uncased chorizo meat (sometimes labeled "bulk"), just buy links and squeeze the meat out of the casings.

In a medium saucepan or high-walled sauté pan (not nonstick), combine the chorizo, chili oil, shallot, cinnamon, star anise, and cloves and heat over medium-high heat until the oil reaches 300°F. Reduce the heat to lower the oil temperature to 250°F. Cook, stirring occasionally and adjusting the heat, if necessary, to maintain a temperature of roughly 250°F, until the chorizo becomes dark and crispy, about 45 minutes. If the shallots start to blacken, remove them with a slotted spoon or spider and discard.

Strain the oil through a fine-mesh sieve into a heat-safe container, pressing on the solids to extract as much oil as you can. Drain the chorizo bits on paper towels and remove and discard the spices; transfer the chorizo to a separate airtight container. Store the oil and chorizo in the refrigerator; the chorizo should be eaten within 1 week and the oil will keep for up to 6 months. When cooled, the oil will solidify, which is normal. To reheat the bits of chorizo, just sauté them quickly in a small nonstick skillet (no need to add more oil).

Szechuan-Spiced Maple Syrup

Makes about 2 cups

2 cups pure maple syrup
¼ cup Szechuan peppercorns
1 to 2 cups dried Szechuan chilies (or any fresh hot red chili), chopped (quantity depends on desired spice level)

Originally made to pair with my Hong Kong Chicken and Waffles (page 245), this spiced maple syrup is a great warming addition to sweet breakfasts like pancakes and makes a contrasting garnish for savory fall dishes like roasted sweet potatoes or kabocha squash. Using the technique here, try out your own combinations of whole spices instead of, or in addition to, the Szechuan pepper. Any of the spices that make up Chinese Five-Spice Powder (page 59) or garam masala will work well.

In a small saucepan, bring the maple syrup to a simmer over medium heat. Add the peppercorns and cook for 5 minutes, reducing the heat to low if it looks like it will boil over. Add the chilies and cook, tasting every 5 minutes, until the syrup reaches your desired spice level; it will become spicier the longer it simmers. Strain through a fine-mesh sieve into a heat-safe container (discard the solids). Store in the refrigerator for up to 1 week or in the freezer for up to 3 months. Warm before serving.

Clockwise from top left:
Szechuan-Spiced Maple Syrup (page 48), Chinese Chimichurri (page 50), Garlic Honey (page 51), Tomato Soy Sauce (page 52).

Broths, Condiments, Spice Blends, and an All-Purpose Egg

Chinese Chimichurri

Makes about 1½ cups

3 garlic cloves, peeled
2 teaspoons kosher salt
2 cups packed fresh parsley
  leaves
Leaves from 4 sprigs oregano
¼ cup Ginger Scallion Oil
  (page 53), raw or cooked
2 teaspoons Fragrant Chili Oil
  (page 45) or Basic Chili Oil
  (page 44)
2 teaspoons white wine vinegar

Chimichurri is a sharp Argentinean condiment made from herbs and garlic that is most often drizzled over grilled beef. I always wondered why prime cuts of meat were absent in American Chinese cooking and suspect that the stereotype of it being a cheaper cuisine hindered the use of more expensive ingredients such as prime steak (rib eye, tenderloin, etc.). That led me to think about what in the Chinese culinary sphere would make a good steak sauce, and I decided ginger scallion oil would be a good base for a chimichurri-inspired sauce. Also, "Chinese chimichurri" (or "chimichurri Chino," as it would be in Spanish) is just a lot of fun to say.

Using the fragrant chili oil here gives the best flavor, especially since I like to include a lot of the chunky bits from the oil for even more pops of flavor, but you can use basic chili oil if that's all you have. Use this chimichurri to marinate protein or finish grilled steak, chicken, lamb, or duck, or even large grilled mushrooms.

Roughly chop the garlic on a cutting board, sprinkle with the salt, and mince until it's almost a paste. Add the parsley and oregano and mince the herbs into the garlic until the mixture is very fine.

Transfer to a medium bowl and add the ginger scallion oil, chili oil, and vinegar. Refrigerate for at least 1 hour to let the flavors meld before using. Store in an airtight container in the fridge for up to 3 days.

Garlic Honey

Makes 1 cup

1 cup honey
5 garlic cloves, grated
½ teaspoon kosher salt

This is a savory-sweet condiment that kinda brings me back to eating Chinese takeout when I lived in Canada. I came up with the recipe to serve with fried chicken wings for my first pop-ups in Detroit. It's excellent with anything deep-fried, from the obvious fried chicken to pork ribs, wontons, spring rolls . . . you name it.

In a small saucepan, heat the honey over medium heat until it starts to steam and bubble around the edges. Add the garlic and salt, stir until the salt dissolves, then remove from the heat and let stand for about 15 minutes to allow the flavors to infuse the honey. Let cool, then transfer to an airtight container (there's no need to strain out the garlic before using, but you can if you want) and store in the fridge for up to 1 month.

The great thing about condiments is that you're welcome to try them with whatever you think they'd taste good with. Most don't just go on any one thing.

Tomato Soy Sauce

Makes about 6 cups

4 pounds very (or over) ripe
    peak-of-season tomatoes,
    any type (about 8)
4 cups light soy sauce

Once at the end of tomato season at my farmers' market, I saw twenty-pound baskets of tomatoes for $15. I came up with this recipe as a way to use all those tomatoes: a summery soy sauce that lasts me through the winter. Use this in place of regular soy sauce when you're looking for a little extra depth of umami flavor. It's also delicious as a simple finishing condiment over almost any rice or noodle dish—think of it as soy sauce, just not as salty, and with even more umami from the tomato. This recipe multiplies easily; use one pound of tomatoes per 1 cup soy sauce.

Crush the tomatoes with your hands and drop them into a large saucepan or Dutch oven. (They don't have to be thoroughly crushed since you'll mash them later.) Add the soy sauce and bring to a simmer over medium heat. Simmer, stirring occasionally, until the tomatoes soften and fall apart, about 10 minutes. Use a potato masher or wooden spoon to crush the tomatoes in the pan, incorporating them into the soy sauce as much as possible. Cover and cook for 10 minutes more to further blend the flavors. Set aside to cool.

Strain the sauce through a fine-mesh strainer into a bowl, using a spoon or rubber spatula to press on the solids to extract as much liquid as possible (discard the solids). Transfer to a jar or other airtight container and store in the fridge for up to 6 months.

Ginger Scallion Oil
(Raw or Cooked)

Makes about 3 cups

2 cups finely minced scallions
2 teaspoons kosher salt
½ cup finely minced fresh ginger
2 cups neutral oil

Note: Salt your scallions before adding oil. It's hard to season oil with salt so we add salt to the scallions, which releases water, which then dissolves the salt, which finally coats and is reabsorbed by the scallions.

If there were master sauces in Chinese cookery, ginger scallion oil would be one of them. Used as a condiment for nearly everything, it is universally loved and super easy to make. There are two main types: raw and cooked. The cooked version is a little less pungent and keeps in the fridge for about a week, while the raw oil should be used the same day you make it. Make both and choose your favorite. Then make it again (and again).

To make raw ginger scallion oil: Place the scallions and salt (see Note) in a large bowl and mix well with a large spoon, then add the ginger and mix again. Stir in the oil, then place the bowl in the refrigerator and let steep for at least 2 hours or up to 12 hours before using. Use within 1 day of making.

To make cooked ginger scallion oil: Place the scallions and salt in a large heat-safe bowl and mix well with a large spoon before adding the ginger and mixing again. In a saucepan, heat the oil over medium-high heat until it reaches 300°F. Slowly pour the oil into the bowl over the scallion mixture and stir to combine. Let cool to room temperature, then transfer to an airtight container and store in the fridge for up to 1 week.

Kung Food

Duo Jiao
(Fermented Chili Paste)

Makes about 5 cups

3 pounds (1,360 grams) fresh
red chilies (I use cayenne)
20 garlic cloves, peeled
1 cup chopped fresh ginger
68 grams pickling salt (see Note,
page 56)
¼ cup plus 1 tablespoon vodka,
plus more as needed

A three-week fermentation process tones down the harsh spice of fresh chilies, making a pungent and briny condiment that transforms simple dishes like steamed fish, grilled vegetables, or fried eggs over rice into a complex restaurant-style dish. The process of making duo jiao is similar to that for making kimchi or sauerkraut: Salt draws moisture from the chilies and preserves them while maintaining an environment where beneficial bacteria can thrive. I use thin red cayenne peppers for this, because that's what's easily available and affordable near me, but any fresh hot chili can be used. You can use any color chilies, but I prefer using all red, as crushing red and green chilies together gets you something brownish—sticking to red gives you the visual drama you deserve.

As with anything fermented, some patience and care are required here. Make sure your tools and containers are sterilized. A fermentation crock is ideal, although you can easily turn a mason jar with a new band and lid into a fermentation vessel (glass jars can always be sterilized and reused, but the lids and bands should be new). Traditionally the Chinese liquor baijiu is used here, but I've substituted vodka, rum, cognac, and even scotch with minimal difference in results; the minor flavor variations are more novel than objectionable. Because fermentation is a delicate process and one in which you invest a great deal of time, and because pickling salts can vary in density, I insist that you measure the salt by weight, not volume; 68 grams is 5 percent the weight of the chilies. I highly recommend that you use the gram measurements to make this recipe. You can easily add too much salt with cup or spoon measures, resulting in an inedible, oversalted paste that accidentally kills all the beneficial bacteria, which is the whole point of making this dish in the first place.

Pull the stems from the chilies, making sure to remove only the stem and none of the chili (i.e., don't slice them open at the stem) and throwing away any that are soft, bruised, or showing signs of rot.

(recipe continues)

Duo Jiao (Fermented Chile Paste) (cont.)

Note: Pickling salt is also known as canning or preserving salt. It's a pure, fine salt that dissolves quickly and contains no anticaking agents or chemicals (such as iodine) that can affect the pickling process. You can find it in many large grocery stores and online.

Wash the chilies under running water to remove any dust or dirt, then set them in a single layer on a wire rack or baking sheet in the sun to dry completely. If it's not sunny, you can put them in a food dehydrator or in the oven on its lowest setting with the door open for an hour. The point is just to eliminate every bit of surface moisture, not dehydrate them completely.

Place the garlic and ginger in a food processor and process to a paste. Add the chilies and process until they're chopped very finely but not yet a smooth purée.

In a large bowl, wearing gloves, use your hands to mix the chili mixture with the pickling salt and vodka, mixing well enough that the salt comes in contact with every part of the chilies. (I find this is easier to do with your hands, but if you don't have gloves, you can use two large clean spoons.)

Pour some vodka into a clean spray bottle (if you don't have a spray bottle, use a paper towel dipped into vodka) and spray the inside of your fermentation vessel (for this recipe, one that holds about 6 cups is ideal), then use a clean cloth to wipe down every interior surface. Pack the vessel tightly with the chili mixture, then sterilize any exposed portion of the jar with vodka. Packing tightly is important, as any open space in the vessel is a potential growth area for mold, so it's best to make sure as much of the vessel is filled with the salty mixture as possible. Store at room temperature (if your vessel is clear, store it in a dark place) for 3 weeks; don't open the container during this time. At three weeks, the aroma should be full and complex; appetizing with a slight hint of acidity. If it smells bad—like cheese or rotting food—or there is any sign of mold, you'll have to toss that batch and start over.

Transfer the vessel to the fridge to stop the fermenting. It will keep in the fridge, tightly covered, for up to 6 months.

Broths, Condiments, Spice Blends, and an All-Purpose Egg

Kung Food

Five-Spice Powder

Makes about ¼ cup

8 star anise pods
5 whole cloves
3 cinnamon sticks
1 tablespoon Szechuan
   peppercorns
1 tablespoon fennel seeds

The components of five-spice powder are among the most important spices in Chinese braises, broths, and sauces. Mixed together, the spice blend becomes a handy all-purpose seasoning that can play dominant or background roles in savory and sweet dishes. As with all spice blends, the homemade version (instead of store-bought) is way more potent and vibrant in aroma and flavor. It also lets you play with the individual amount of each ingredient, so you can customize the blend to your preferences.

In a wok or skillet, toast the star anise, cloves, and cinnamon over medium heat, stirring often, until they start to release their aromas, about 3 minutes. Add the Szechuan peppercorns and fennel seeds and toast, stirring continuously, until wisps of white smoke start to come from the pan and the fennel starts to change color, another 1 to 2 minutes. Transfer the spices to a baking sheet or plate and let cool completely (grinding warm spices can make a sticky powder that clumps or is hard to remove from the grinder).

Using a spice grinder or mortar and pestle, grind the spices to a fine powder. Store in an airtight container in a cool, dark, and dry place; it will keep its full potency for about a month and will keep in the cupboard for at least a year, though after a few months it becomes similar to store-bought in flavor.

Cumin-Based
Five-Spice Powder

Makes about 6 tablespoons

2 teaspoons allspice berries
3 tablespoons cumin seeds
1 tablespoon fennel seeds
1 tablespoon coriander seeds
⅓ cup dried curry leaves

This is a spice blend for lovers of the earthy, full flavor of cumin, like myself. It can be used anywhere that calls for traditional five-spice powder. Try mixing this with salt to use as a rub on stronger-flavored meats like lamb, duck, and goat or sprinkle on mushrooms as you're stir-frying them or blocks of tempeh as you flip them over a grill. Most of these spices are somewhat delicate, so use a gentle touch when toasting them.

In a wok or skillet, toast the allspice over medium heat, stirring often, until it starts to release its aromas, about 3 minutes. Quickly add the cumin, fennel, and coriander and stir until they release their aromas, about 30 seconds, then add the curry leaves. Cook, stirring often, until wisps of white smoke start to come from the pan, about 30 seconds. Transfer the spices to a baking sheet or plate and let cool completely.

Using a spice grinder or mortar and pestle, grind the cooled spices to a fine powder. Store in an airtight container or jar in a cool, dark, and dry place; it will retain its full potency for about a month and will keep in the cupboard for at least a year, though it diminishes in potency after a few months.

Bright Five-Spice Powder

Makes about ¼ cup

1 black cardamom pod
2 tablespoons Szechuan
   peppercorns
2 large pieces dried mandarin
   orange peel
2 teaspoons coriander seeds
1 teaspoon (or a pinkie-tip-size
   nub) dried sand ginger

The bright and subtly smoky-sweet elements of orange peel and the sweetness of coriander seeds make this version of five-spice especially delicious on fish, as well as on meats that will end up in spicy dishes, because the blend also offers a nice contrast to bold and intense flavors. To learn more about any of these spices, check out the pantry section on page 22.

Crack open the cardamom pod with the flat side of a chef's knife, remove the tiny seeds, and discard the pod.

In a sauté pan or wok, toast the cardamom, Szechuan peppercorns, orange peel, coriander, and sand ginger over medium heat, stirring continuously, until they release their aromas and wisps of white smoke start to come from the pan, about 3 minutes. Transfer the spices to a baking sheet or plate and let cool completely.

Using a spice grinder or mortar and pestle, grind the spices to a fine powder. Store in an airtight container or jar in a cool, dark, and dry place; it will keep its full potency for about a month and will keep in the cupboard for at least a year, though it diminishes in potency after a few months.

The Sous Vide Poached Egg

Makes 12 sous vide poached eggs (as long as you don't break any)

12 large eggs

We had buckets of these on hand at one of the restaurants I worked at. I topped our steak tartare with them, but I quicky found that having the eggs at the ready is such a blessing to a bowl of rice or noodles. That's why I included the recipe in this book, even if it requires an immersion circulator (some newer automatic pressure cookers have a sous vide option as well). If you sous vide a dozen of these eggs, cool them, and put them back in the fridge in a (marked) egg carton, you have a week's access to super-soft, beautifully mixable cooked eggs that can be added as an afterthought to rice, noodles, and soups without any advance preparation. It's just one of those restaurant prep hacks where you do a little work now so it's ready to go at mealtime. Use these to top any noodle dish or rice bowl, or to add some protein to any congee in this book.

Follow the instructions for your immersion circulator to create a 145°F water bath. Once it reaches that temperature, carefully drop in the whole eggs. Poach for 1 hour 15 minutes to 2 hours. The longer they cook, the thicker and fudgier the yolks will be, while the white will always be a little soft and liquid-y. (It's a little like the reverse of soft-boiled eggs, with their firm whites and liquid yolks.)

Fill a large bowl with ice and water. Using a slotted spoon or spider, transfer the eggs to the ice bath to stop the cooking, then place them back in the carton. Mark the carton in a way that tells you the eggs inside are cooked (or mark each egg with a Sharpie or pencil) and place them back in the fridge. They will keep for up to a week.

To use the eggs, just crack one into a piping-hot bowl of rice or noodles, which will both reheat the egg and bring the dish to an immediately consumable temperature (peak home-cooking laziness right there). If you'd like to warm the egg first, fill a glass with your hottest tap water and put the egg in there for at least 3 minutes before cracking it. A warmed egg won't bring down the temperature of the dish, and it often allows the hot dish to cook the egg white a little further.

Broths, Condiments, Spice Blends, and an All-Purpose Egg

Snacky Snacks, Bites, and Cravings

When describing my childhood eating habits, my mom would tell her friends that I was born in the year of the rat, which is why I ate like one. She was referring to my habit of scurrying around the house when no one was around and snacking on anything and everything I could get my hands on. I would also bring wrapped treats, like a chocolate bar or hard candy, back to my bed and eat under the covers, leaving wrappers as evidence for my parents to find while I was at school. For all my snacking, I was still able to eat at the dinner table as if nothing happened.

I still love snacking, though my definition of what makes a snack has changed over the years. This chapter covers things that I find myself whipping up quickly to eat in front of the TV, before or after working out, to serve with drinks when I have friends over, or just to keep in the fridge all week for when I need a quick fix. With buns and sandwiches, hearty salads, and even a drink, any of these foods can be part of a meal, but they can also be a meal in and of themselves. Feel free to mix and match them with anything else in the book.

Kung Food

Sesame Shrimp Toast

Makes 4 toasts

Shrimp paste

8 ounces peeled and deveined
  raw shrimp (any size)
2 garlic cloves, roughly chopped
1 teaspoon grated fresh ginger
2 teaspoons light soy sauce
2 teaspoons toasted sesame oil
1 teaspoon oyster sauce
½ teaspoon freshly ground white
  pepper
½ teaspoon smoked paprika
1 teaspoon cornstarch
1 large egg white
2 scallions, thinly sliced
1 carrot, brunoised (¼ cup;
  optional)
1 celery stalk, brunoised (¼ cup;
  optional)
¼ cup brunoised canned water
  chestnuts (optional)

Toasts

4 thin slices soft white sandwich
  bread
1 tablespoon untoasted hulled
  sesame seeds
Neutral oil

Though "toast" (in the sense of something beyond buttered bread) really came into the American culinary zeitgeist with the millennial generation, in Hong Kong it's been a teatime staple for decades, ever since British imperialists introduced bread to the island. Locals assimilated it into their own food culture, and soon enough shrimp toast—what I suspect was just shrimp dumpling filling spread over a slice of bread and pan-fried—had become a ubiquitous and quintessential Hong Kong dish. While totally optional, the brunoised vegetables—especially the water chestnuts—provide a nice crispness and textural contrast to the rich paste.

Make the shrimp paste: In a food processor, combine the shrimp, garlic, ginger, soy sauce, sesame oil, oyster sauce, white pepper, and paprika and blitz into a paste. Add the cornstarch and egg white and pulse to fully combine. Transfer to a medium bowl and stir in the scallions and the carrot, celery, and water chestnuts (if using). Transfer the shrimp paste to a bowl, cover with plastic wrap, and refrigerate for at least 30 minutes and up to 24 hours.

Make the toasts: When ready to cook, spread the shrimp paste over one side of each slice of bread, dividing it evenly among them and making sure to fully and evenly cover the entire surface. Sprinkle evenly with the sesame seeds.

There's no need to pretoast the sesame seeds—they will toast up when you fry them.

(recipe continues)

Generously coat a cast-iron or other heavy skillet with oil and heat over medium heat until the oil is shimmering or a sesame seed sizzles on contact. Add the bread, seed-side down, and press down on it gently with the back of a spatula to help the seeds adhere as they cook. Cook for about 3 minutes, just until the shrimp paste is cooked through and the sesame seeds turn golden brown; reduce the heat if the seeds start to burn. Flip and cook until brown on the other side, about 1 minute more. Serve immediately.

Variation: Shrimp Meatballs

If you form the shrimp paste into balls and toss them into a pot of gently boiling water, they become meatballs. Once cooked, they'll gingerly float and bob at the top. Remove them using a slotted spoon, stick some toothpicks in them, and serve them as hors d'oeuvres so your carb-free friends feel included. Serve with a little black vinegar on the side. You can also use this paste as a filling for dumplings (see page 157).

68

Sweet Sesame Pumpkin Toast

Makes 2 toasts

1 to 1½ pounds kabocha squash, seeded

Olive oil (optional)

4 tablespoons (½ stick) unsalted butter

1 tablespoon Five-Spice Powder (page 59) or garam masala

1 teaspoon sugar or pure maple syrup

Kosher salt

¼ cup chopped walnuts or pecans

1 teaspoon grated orange zest (optional)

2 (1-inch-thick) slices brioche, challah, or sourdough bread

1 tablespoon untoasted hulled sesame seeds, plus more if needed

Kabocha is Japanese for pumpkin.

This sweet fall-inspired toast makes use of one of my favorite squashes—kabocha. The Japanese call most winter squashes kabocha, while in Hong Kong and Australia kabocha is referred to as simply "pumpkin." In the US it's sold as kabocha squash. It's a taste that's somewhere in between pumpkin and sweet potato and has a wonderfully creamy texture. Kabocha is perfect for both sweet and savory applications, like curries, soups, spreads—I smear this on toast—and pies.

Cook the squash by either steaming or roasting: To steam, cut the squash into 2-inch pieces. Set a steamer basket over a pot of simmering water, put the squash in the steamer, cover, and steam for 30 to 45 minutes. To roast, cut the squash into 1- to 1½-inch pieces, toss in a little olive oil, and roast in a single layer on a parchment-lined baking sheet at 375°F for 45 minutes. In both cases, cook until the squash can be easily mashed with a fork. Remove from the steamer or the oven and let cool.

When cool enough to handle, remove the skin from the squash pieces and put the flesh in a bowl. Add 1 tablespoon of the butter and mash with a fork or potato masher until smooth. Stir in the five-spice, sugar, and salt to taste. Next, stir in the nuts and orange zest (if using).

Spread the squash mixture thickly over one side of each slice of bread, covering it from edge to edge. Sprinkle with the sesame seeds in a single layer to cover the surface (you may need additional sesame seeds, depending on the size of the bread).

In a large nonstick skillet, melt the remaining 3 tablespoons butter over medium-high heat until it's sizzling. Add the toasts, seed-side down, and cook until browned and fragrant but not burned, about 3 minutes (if they start to burn, turn down the heat). Flip and cook until brown on the other side, about 1 minute more. Serve immediately.

Condensed Milk on Toast

Serves 1

Thick-sliced bread (preferably
Japanese milk bread or white
bread)
Salted butter
Sweetened condensed milk
Strong black tea or coffee, for
serving

This isn't so much a recipe as just a simple sweet snack to go with your strong black tea (or coffee). I loved this as a kid.

In a toaster or toaster oven, toast the bread to a deep golden brown, spread with butter to taste, drizzle with condensed milk to taste, and enjoy with a cup of strong black tea or coffee.

Condensed milk really is that girl. If you see her in a recipe you know it's gonna be *lush.*

Snacky Snacks, Bites, and Cravings

Kung Food

Shredded Chicken Breast
+ 3 Chicken Salads

**Makes about 2 cups
shredded chicken**

Kosher salt

2 scallions, roughly chopped

1 thumb-size piece fresh ginger, peeled and thinly sliced

1 teaspoon Szechuan peppercorns

2 boneless, skinless chicken breasts (about 6 ounces each), fresh or frozen (no need to thaw)

Optional aromatics: smashed garlic cloves, rosemary sprigs, star anise pods, bruised lemongrass stalks, fresh or dried sand ginger

As a person who's pretty focused on fitness, I can't deny the convenience and efficiency of chicken breast as a protein source (even though I occasionally go out of my way to bash it in my videos). So I took a page from Chinese and Vietnamese pulled chicken salads, which are both moist and flavorful, and actually really tasty. You can make this with chicken breasts direct from the freezer, making it an even more convenient choice.

Having pulled chicken in the fridge gives me easy access to a quick meal component—just add greens, stuff it into a pita or butter lettuce leaf, or pile it on top of noodles or rice. Toss it in with Ginger Scallion Oil (page 53), Duo Jiao (page 55), or any of the congee fixings on page 195 to bring some excitement to a normally rather plain ingredient.

Can you also buy a rotisserie chicken and save the breasts for this purpose? Or use leftover grilled chicken? Of course you can, silly goose.

Fill a medium saucepan about half full with water and stir in enough salt that it tastes pleasantly (not overly) salty, you can also use light or Japanese soy sauce. Add the scallions, ginger, Szechuan peppercorns, and any optional aromatics you have on hand, and bring to a boil over high heat.

Add the chicken, return the water to a boil, then reduce the heat to medium-low to maintain a light simmer, meaning a few bubbles come to the surface every few seconds. Cook for 5 minutes if the chicken is fresh, or 20 minutes if you're cooking from frozen, then check the temperature in the thickest part using a meat thermometer. When it hits 150°F (see Note), turn the heat off and leave the chicken in the hot water for another 10 minutes. Transfer the chicken to a plate and set aside until it's cool enough to handle with your bare hands.

(recipe continues)

Hand-pull the chicken into larger strips (much like pulling string cheese) or use two forks to shred it. I prefer it hand-pulled, as it's more texturally interesting. If you're working with a large batch for meal prep you can also put the breasts in the bowl of a stand mixer fitted with the paddle attachment and beat on low speed to shred the meat, which will take only a few seconds; pulling out the mixer for a couple of breasts isn't worth the time you'll spend doing the extra dishes, but I think it is for three or more breasts. Store the cooked chicken breast in a tightly covered container in the refrigerator for up to 3 days.

Note: The USDA recommends cooking chicken to an internal temperature of 165°F because bacteria are instantly killed at that temperature; however, they're also killed at 150°F if the meat is held at that temp for 3 minutes or longer. As the chicken sits in the hot liquid, carryover cooking will increase or maintain the internal temperature, so it will easily be at least 150°F for at least 3 minutes. Doing this produces a juicier chicken breast, which would otherwise have ended up chalky and dry if cooked to 165°F.

Spicy Chicken Salad

Serves 4

It's like a chicken salad, but spicy.

---

2 cups shredded or pulled cooked chicken breast
    (see page 73)
½ cup fresh cilantro leaves
¼ cup thinly sliced scallions
2 tablespoons Fragrant Chili Oil (page 45)
1 teaspoon light soy sauce
1 teaspoon toasted hulled sesame seeds
2 cups chopped romaine lettuce or cubed
    cucumbers (or both; live your life)
Pitas, for serving (optional)

In a large bowl, combine the chicken, cilantro,
scallions, chili oil, soy sauce, and sesame seeds and
toss to combine. Add the lettuce and/or cucumbers
and toss again to coat. Serve as a salad or stuffed
into pitas (if using).

Duo Jiao Chicken Salad

Serves 4

*This chicken salad takes advantage of the complex
flavor of duo jiao, a fermented chili paste that
tastes deep, salty, and mildly spicy. A touch of
vinegar and sweetness round it out, while cilantro
adds color and a burst of freshness (sub sliced
scallions if you're averse to cilantro). This can be
served as is, stuffed in a pita as a sandwich, piled
on top of a bed of greens, or as the tasty protein in
a bowl of rice or congee.*

---

2 cups shredded or pulled cooked chicken breast
    (see page 73)
2 tablespoons Zhenjiang black vinegar
2 tablespoons light soy sauce
1 tablespoon Duo Jiao (page 55)
1 teaspoon sugar
1 cup fresh cilantro leaves or 2 whole scallions,
    thinly sliced

In a large bowl, combine the chicken, vinegar, soy
sauce, duo jiao, sugar, and cilantro. Toss and serve.

(recipe continues)

Asian Chicken Salad

Serves 4

Margaret Cho had this amazing bit about a flight attendant serving "Asian chicken salad" on a plane and freezing up when he got to her seat, as if she'd be terribly offended. It was such a funny way to highlight the ridiculousness of how monolithic stereotypes are applied to us in open commerce. These sorts of generic, watered-down "Asian fusion" dishes seem silly today but also a little iconic in their foolishness. For the sake of matching that audacity, I had to make a version for myself. Let an Asian have a stab at this salad for a change.

2 tablespoons extra-virgin olive oil

1 tablespoon store-bought ponzu (a citrus and soy-based sauce)

1 teaspoon sugar

2 cups shredded or pulled cooked chicken breast (see page 73)

1 teaspoon Basic Szechuan Peppercorn Oil (page 46)

Kosher salt and freshly ground black pepper

5 cups loosely packed arugula

¼ pomelo or 1 pink grapefruit, suprêmed (see Note, page 79)

½ cup shelled unsalted pistachios or walnuts, toasted, and roughly chopped

In a small bowl, whisk together the olive oil, ponzu, and sugar until the sugar dissolves (you can also shake this up in a jar).

In a separate large bowl, toss the chicken with the Szechuan peppercorn oil and salt and pepper to taste. Add the arugula, citrus suprêmes, and nuts to the bowl and toss to combine. Add the ponzu mixture and toss to coat everything evenly. Taste and add more salt and pepper, if needed, and serve as a main-course salad.

(recipe continues)

Snacky Snacks, Bites, and Cravings

Kung Food

Note: To make citrus suprêmes, cut away the top and bottom of the citrus to create a flat surface and expose the fruit. Stand the citrus upright on a cutting board and, following the curve of the fruit, slice from top to bottom to remove the peel and pith (the bitter white part), exposing the flesh. Working over a bowl, hold the fruit in one hand and use a sharp paring knife to cut each segment away from the membrane on either side, letting the segments and juice fall into the bowl, then discard the membrane. You can also find packaged suprêmed grapefruit at some supermarkets (as someone who spent an hour suprêming fruit daily when I worked in restaurants, seeing them sitting precut on a shelf affected me deeply). Pomelos, however, usually can be simply peeled clean.

Pomelos are large, usually at least twice as big as a grapefruit. One segment can easily be split into two to three parts and distributed in this salad. They're also very mild, so even if you use a lot more, you don't have to worry about them overpowering the rest of the dish.

Crushed Cucumber Salad
with Shanxi Vinaigrette

Serves 2 to 4

2 tablespoons Shanxi or
    Zhenjiang black vinegar
1 tablespoon light soy sauce
2 teaspoons sugar
1 garlic clove, smashed
2 or 3 dried Szechuan chilies,
    sliced (optional)
¼ cup olive oil
2 English cucumbers

Maybe it's because of their bulk, but cucumber salads are so much more satisfying to me than just leafy greens. Crushing the cucumbers with your fist (or the flat side of a cleaver) allows for better absorption of the dressing and softens the texture of the cucumber a little, too. Shanxi vinegar is a long-aged multigrain black vinegar from Shanxi Province, available online and in larger Chinese groceries. Zhenjiang vinegar, which is more easily found outside China, is an acceptable substitute.

In a large bowl, whisk together the vinegar, soy sauce, sugar, garlic, and chilies (if using) until the sugar dissolves. While whisking, slowly pour in the olive oil and whisk until emulsified (the dressing ingredients can also be shaken in a jar until the sugar dissolves). Remove the garlic clove, or don't. You can make the dressing days ahead; you can keep it in a jar and shake to emulsify right before mixing it in.

Wrap cucumbers in plastic wrap or a clean towel before smashing. Pound the cucumbers with your fist firmly enough that the skin breaks but gently enough that the flesh doesn't burst out of the plastic wrap. Remove the plastic and cut off and discard the ends of the cucumbers. Cut the cucumbers in half lengthwise, then slice them crosswise into bite-size pieces. Add them to the dressing and toss to evenly coat, then serve. (If you're making this ahead, wait until the last moment to dress the cucumbers, since they'll continue to absorb dressing over time, eventually making them too sour and salty.)

English cucumbers tend to be sold individually wrapped in plastic. If you keep the plastic on when you lightly smash them, you'll minimize the mess.

Snacky Snacks, Bites, and Cravings

Kung Food

Wood Ear or Black Fungus Mushroom Salad

Serves 4

1 cup dried wood ear or black fungus (cloud ear) mushrooms

1 tablespoon Zhenjiang black vinegar

1 teaspoon toasted sesame oil

1 teaspoon sugar

1 teaspoon light soy sauce

2 fresh red chilies (such as Thai, cayenne, or Fresno), stemmed and sliced (optional)

1 garlic clove, smashed

1 cup fresh cilantro leaves

1 tablespoon toasted hulled sesame seeds

¼ cup fried sliced garlic, or ½ cup fried sliced shallots (see Note, page 84)

Both wood ear and black fungus (or cloud ear) mushrooms have a similar dark brown color and a gelatinous, pleasantly floppy texture when reconstituted from their dried state. Wood ears tend to be thicker and more rounded, almost resembling the shape of human ears, while black fungus has a bursting floral shape with ruffles. They're very closely related, have only the slightest textural differences, and can be used interchangeably in dishes.

These dried mushrooms need to be soaked before eating—while technically they can be consumed raw (provided they are clean and were grown in a sterilized environment), blanching them briefly in boiling water makes them easier to digest. By soaking them ahead of time and storing in the fridge, you can put this dish together really quickly. Feel free to add shredded cooked chicken breast (see page 73) for a more filling and protein-rich snack. You can also use dried mushrooms in a stir-fry or mince them and add them to a dumpling filling.

Put the mushrooms in a large bowl and cover with plenty of water. Set aside at room temperature for 2 hours or, for the best springy texture, refrigerate overnight. (Some use boiling water to save time, but this only shaves off about an hour and causes the mushrooms to lose some of their appealing bounce.) Drain the mushrooms; sometimes they have hard stems, so after soaking, use a knife or kitchen shears to remove any you find. (If you aren't using the mushrooms immediately, refrigerate them in a covered container for up to a week.)

Bring a large pot of water to a boil over high heat. Add the soaked mushrooms and cook for 4 minutes, then drain and let cool to room temperature.

(recipe continues)

Note: You can purchase fried garlic and fried shallots at many Southeast Asian grocery stores. While they lack the crisp sweetness of the home-fried version, they're still better than nothing, and are a versatile enough topping to put on nearly anything savory you make from this book, especially congee, rice bowls, or noodles.

While the mushrooms cook, in a large bowl, whisk together the vinegar, sesame oil, sugar, soy sauce, and chilies (if using) until the sugar dissolves, then add the garlic and let stand so the garlic absorbs into the dressing.

Discard the garlic clove from the dressing (or not; I don't), add the mushrooms to the bowl, and toss to coat. Gently stir in the cilantro leaves so they're evenly distributed and don't fall to the bottom of the bowl.

Transfer the mushrooms to a serving dish and garnish with the sesame seeds and fried garlic or shallots. Serve immediately. This salad, minus the cilantro and garnishes, can be stored in a covered container in the refrigerator for up to 3 days.

Steamed Yuk Bang

Serves 4

1 pound ground beef (preferably 85% lean), ground pork, or plant-based ground meat alternative

1 tablespoon grated fresh ginger

2 garlic cloves, grated

1 tablespoon Shaoxing wine

1 teaspoon light soy sauce

2 teaspoons whole white peppercorns, toasted and ground

1 teaspoon cornstarch

½ teaspoon kosher salt

⅛ teaspoon baking soda

4 scallions, thinly sliced

Steamed rice, for serving

Yuk bang, which translates to "meat cake," is a steamed meat dish (with ginger and garlic added here for punch); a friend described it as "sort of a steamed meat loaf, but in the best possible way." While it might sound a little odd (albeit no odder than "meat loaf"), steaming is a common method of cooking ground meats in China, and it is a healthy way to prepare meat to serve as a companion to rice. This also works beautifully with vegan ground meat replacements. Serve over rice with dark soy sauce, black vinegar, Duo Jiao (page 55), or Fragrant Chili Oil (page 45) as condiments. A steamer basket is essential for this recipe, so if you don't have one yet, grab one. It's a humble-looking dish, but it's tasty, healthy, relatively easy, and absolutely worth a slot in your weeknight repertoire.

Set up a wok with a steaming base or place a large steamer basket over a pot of boiling water. (The former is best for this recipe because it makes the plate easier to remove and minimizes the mess.)

Lotus Root Yuk Bang

Try sandwiching the yuk bang patties between thin slices of lotus root, pressing gently so the meat mixture goes into the holes of the lotus root. Check after steaming for 8 to 10 minutes; oversteamed ground meat feels like rubber. If you're buying fresh lotus root, peel it—or just give the surface a good scrub (I never peel mine)—and slice it crosswise no more than ¼ inch thick.

In a large bowl, using a wooden spoon or clean hands, mix the ground meat, ginger, garlic, wine, soy sauce, white pepper, cornstarch, salt, baking soda, and half the scallions until everything is well incorporated.

On a plate that fits into your wok or steamer basket, press the meat mixture into a single large flat patty— I usually make it about ½ inch thick. Place the plate in the steamer, cover, and steam until the meat is cooked through, about 8 to 12 minutes (the timing will depend on the thickness of your meat patty).

Serve immediately over rice, garnished with the remaining scallions and with condiments passed separately.

Pork Chop Buns

Makes 4 buns

4 (6-ounce) boneless pork chops
2 garlic cloves, grated
¼ cup light soy sauce
2 tablespoons Shaoxing wine
1 teaspoon toasted sesame oil
2 tablespoons freshly ground
    white pepper
2 teaspoons Five-Spice Powder
    (page 59)
2 teaspoons cornstarch
Neutral oil, for frying
3 cups panko bread crumbs
3 large egg whites
4 Pão Francês rolls (page 91),
    Mexican bolillos, Portuguese
    buns, or 6-inch sections of
    baguette, split horizontally
    and warmed
½ large red, white, or sweet
    onion, sliced paper-thin
Tonkatsu sauce, for serving

I remember the first time my mom took me to Macau. We ate pork chop buns while perusing the Chinese and Portuguese buildings that stand side by side in the historic city center. Four hundred years of Portuguese colonial rule influenced not only the architecture but the food, too: Macanese cuisine has Cantonese and Portuguese roots, as well as Southeast Asian influences. It was so interesting to see how this Chinese city merged flavors and ingredients to create something new, even as each retained its individual and traditional style. Though the food was like nothing I'd ever eaten, how they got there made perfect sense to me. Any time I travel to a country with a similar colonial story, no matter how foreign and strange the food might seem, I can always see their processes of culinary adaptation. The bridges between cultures were always the most interesting places to me.

Pork chop buns are an iconic Macanese street food. They're usually made with bone-in pork chops, but boneless make for easier eating. After marinating overnight with garlic, Shaoxing wine, and five-spice, they're coated with whipped egg whites, which make a very light and crispy coating. I serve these with tangy tonkatsu sauce, which isn't traditional, but I love it. As a kid less than an hour away in Hong Kong, I would eat the very same style of pork chops when I was younger, but it would be with black vinegar and rice instead of buns.

Place each pork chop between two layers of plastic wrap. Using a meat mallet or heavy pan, pound them to a uniform thickness of about ¼ inch. Transfer the flattened chops to a large (gallon-size) freezer bag.

(recipe continues)

Snacky Snacks, Bites, and Cravings

In a small bowl, stir together the garlic, soy sauce, wine, sesame oil, white pepper, five-spice, and cornstarch until the cornstarch dissolves, then add the mixture to the bag. Seal the bag and slosh it around to ensure even coverage of all the pork. Marinate in the refrigerator for at least 2 hours or up to 12 hours.

Fill a large heavy skillet with neutral oil to a depth of ½ inch and heat over medium heat to 375°F.

Spread the panko over a large plate. Beat the egg whites in a medium bowl until foamy and increased in volume. Remove the pork from the marinade, wipe off the garlic, and set the chops on a plate; discard the marinade. Working with one at a time, coat each pork chop in the egg white, brush off any excess back into the bowl, then evenly coat both sides in the panko and place the breaded chop carefully in the hot oil. Repeat with the remaining chops (they all should fit in a large skillet at once, but if not, cook them in batches—don't overcrowd the pan or they won't crisp properly). Cook until golden brown, about 4 minutes per side. Drain briefly on a paper towel–lined plate or baking sheet.

Put a breaded chop on the bottom half of each roll (if the chops are very large, cut them into 2 or 3 pieces and stack them on the rolls to fit). Dress with the onion and tonkatsu sauce to taste, close the rolls, and serve.

Chicken Curry Cutlet Buns

Makes 4 buns

4 (6-ounce) boneless, skinless chicken breasts
3 tablespoons Ginger Scallion Oil (page 53)
2 tablespoons Muchi (spicy) or Japanese (mild) curry powder
2 teaspoons garam masala (if using Muchi curry powder) or five-spice powder (if using Japanese curry powder)
2 garlic cloves, grated
2 tablespoons grated fresh ginger
1 tablespoon freshly ground black pepper
2 teaspoons toasted sesame oil
2 teaspoons cornstarch
1 teaspoon kosher salt
1½ cups panko bread crumbs
2 large egg whites
Neutral oil, for frying
4 Pão Francês rolls (page 91), Mexican bolillos, Portuguese buns, or 6-inch sections of baguette, split horizontally and warmed

Garnishes and condiments: thinly sliced white onion, sliced Asian pear, bread-and-butter pickles, sharp cheddar, mustard, spicy mayo (it's a sandwich—go nuts)

Here I adapted Japanese chicken curry katsu to the pork bun format. Muchi curry powder will give you a spicier sandwich, while Japanese curry is milder (I particularly like S&B brand Japanese curry). Curry powders are made with raw spices, so I fry them in a bit of oil to activate their flavors—in this recipe, that gets done in the frying process. Never forget to cook your curry powder! You'll be blown away by how much more flavor and nuance comes through in the food.

Place each chicken breast between two layers of plastic wrap. Using a meat mallet or heavy pan, pound them to a uniform thickness of about ¼ inch. Transfer the pounded chicken to a large (gallon-size) freezer bag. In a small bowl, stir together the ginger scallion oil, 1 tablespoon of the curry powder, the garam masala, garlic, ginger, pepper, sesame oil, cornstarch, and salt until the cornstarch dissolves, then add the mixture to the bag. Seal the bag and slosh it around to ensure even coverage of all the chicken. Marinate in the refrigerator for at least 2 hours or up to 12 hours.

Fill a large heavy skillet with neutral oil to a depth of ½ inch and heat over medium heat to 375°F.

Spread the panko over a large plate. Beat the egg whites with the remaining 1 tablespoon curry powder in a large bowl. Remove the chicken breasts from the marinade and wipe off the garlic, ginger, and any other bits that could burn in the oil. Set the chicken on a plate and discard the marinade. Working with one at a time, coat both sides of each chicken breast in the egg white, then evenly coat in the panko and carefully place in the hot oil, taking care not to crowd the pan and working in batches if needed. Cook until golden brown, about 4 minutes per side. Drain briefly on a paper towel–lined plate or baking sheet.

Put a breaded chicken breast on the bottom half of each roll. Dress with garnishes and condiments to taste, close the rolls, and serve.

Kung Food

Pão Francês

Makes 8 medium rolls

3¼ cups bread flour, plus extra
    for dusting
1 tablespoon instant yeast
1 tablespoon sugar
1 teaspoon kosher salt
1½ cups warm water
    (105° to 115°F, a tiny bit
    hotter than a hot tub)
1 tablespoon oil, for greasing

To someone who mainly works with rice and noodles, bread always seemed a daunting thing to me, but these rolls are pretty simple and the payoff of fresh-baked rolls is worth the effort.

In the bowl of a stand mixer fitted with the dough hook, mix the flour, yeast, sugar, and salt until fully incorporated, then add the warm water and mix on the lowest speed until a dough forms. Turn the mixer to medium speed and knead until it is smooth and no longer sticky, about 6 minutes.

Grease a large bowl with oil. Transfer the dough to the oiled bowl, cover with plastic wrap, and set in a warm place in your kitchen to rise until almost doubled in size, about 30 minutes.

Line a baking sheet with parchment paper. Turn the dough out onto a floured work surface and use a bench knife or knife to portion it into 6 pieces. Use a rolling pin to roll out the pieces to equal-size rectangles, about ¼ inch thick, then tightly roll up each rectangle of dough lengthwise like a jelly roll. Place the rolls seam-side down on the lined baking sheet and cover with a clean dish towel. Set aside to rise until almost doubled in size, about an hour.

Preheat the oven to 400°F. Have ready a cup of water and more water in a spray bottle. Place an empty baking sheet or unenameled cast-iron skillet on the bottom shelf (if you have a steam oven, ignore this step).

Use a sharp knife or razor blade to slice a single shallow cut down the length of each roll and give the rolls a mist of water from the spray bottle before putting the pan in the oven. Immediately toss the cup of water onto the empty pan at the bottom of the oven to get a plume of steam going, then shut the oven door immediately. Bake for 15 minutes, or until golden brown. Remove from the oven and set aside to cool. Use immediately or store at room temperature as you would store-bought bread.

SELT (Spam, Egg, Lettuce, and Tomato)

Makes 4 sandwiches

2 tablespoons neutral oil
1 (7-ounce) can Spam, sliced into
    4 pieces
4 large eggs
Softened unsalted butter or
    your favorite sandwich
    condiments (mayo,
    mustard . . .)
4 Pão Francês rolls (page 91),
    Mexican bolillos, Portuguese
    buns, or 6-inch sections of
    baguette, split horizontally
    and warmed
1 beefsteak or large heirloom
    tomato, cut into 8 slices
1 head butter lettuce, leaves
    separated

Spam sandwiches were an after-school snack I always looked forward to as a kid. I especially loved the contrast between the crispy edges of the pan-seared Spam and the squishy, humble white bread; they almost had the subtle elegance of tea sandwiches to me. Building on that, I've added the freshness and substance of fried eggs, crunchy-fresh lettuce, and a juicy tomato slice. (If you can get jalapeño or chorizo Spam, even better.) For my plant-based friends, vegan Spam has been popular in Asia for quite a while and is now available online in the States (I have some in my freezer called OmniPork).

In a large (at least 10-inch-diameter) skillet, heat 1 tablespoon of the oil over medium-high heat. Add the Spam in a single layer and sear until the edges are brown and crispy, about 3 minutes per side. (If using vegan Spam, pan-fry according to the directions on the label.)

In a separate nonstick skillet, heat the remaining 1 tablespoon oil and cook the eggs to your liking (either scrambled or sunny-side up/over easy).

Butter the inside of each roll (or line them with some mayo or mustard—live your life). Add a slice of Spam, then top with an egg, 2 slices of tomato, and a few lettuce leaves. Eat.

BELT (Bacon, [Ginger Scallion] Egg, Lettuce, and Tomato)

Makes 4 sandwiches

8 slices extra-thick-cut bacon (about 1 pound)

⅓ cup Ginger Scallion Oil (page 53), raw or cooked

4 large eggs

Flaky salt

Softened unsalted butter

4 Pão Francês rolls (page 91), Mexican bolillos, Portuguese buns, or 6-inch sections of baguette, split horizontally and warmed

1 beefsteak or large heirloom tomato, cut into 8 slices

1 head butter lettuce, leaves separated

Your favorite sandwich condiments (mayo, mustard, pickles, etc.)

"Everything is better with an egg on it" is a mantra that rarely fails me. And while it does make eating this sandwich a drippy mess, it's completely worth it. Because I'm using the cooked version of the ginger scallion oil, it can withstand additional cooking without losing much of its flavor, but feel free to use raw if that's what you have on hand. Cooking the egg directly in the oil is both beautiful and tasty and is excellent for eggs not destined for a sandwich as well. (Ginger scallion egg on ginger scallion noodles. Yes.) If you can't find extra-thick-cut bacon, you can ask your butcher to cut eight slices from a one-pound slab (or order some online).

Preheat the oven to 400°F. Line a baking sheet with parchment paper and arrange the bacon on the parchment sheet. Bake for 15 to 20 minutes, depending on whether you like it chewy or crispy, then pull it from the oven and let cool. (Tip: Always remove the bacon immediately if you notice lots of white foam coming out of it, as it will burn shortly after this stage.)

Cook the eggs one at a time as follows: In a small nonstick skillet, heat a healthy tablespoon of the ginger scallion oil over medium heat, making sure to get as many of the chunky bits in there as possible. Crack an egg into the hot oil. In a lateral circular motion, gently swirl the egg so the chunky bits from the oil set into the white as it cooks. Once the whites have started to crisp up around the edges and their surface doesn't look liquidy, carefully use a spatula to flip the egg for over easy, or transfer the sunny-side-up egg onto a plate to stop the cooking. Top with a pinch of flaky salt. (Another tip: For an on-the-go sandwich, cook the yolk hard all the way through; otherwise, the runny yolk makes for a messy—but decadent—dish.)

Butter the cut sides of each roll and stuff each with 2 slices of bacon, an egg, 2 slices of tomato, and a few lettuce leaves. Dress with your favorite classic sandwich condiments and serve.

Spicy Fried Oyster Mushroom Sandwich

Makes 4 sandwiches

Neutral oil, for frying
¼ cup Fragrant Chili Oil (page 45)
2 tablespoons Duo Jiao (page 55)
2 teaspoons Five-Spice Powder (page 59), or use store-bought
1 cup potato starch
1 cup all-purpose flour
1 teaspoon freshly ground black pepper
1 teaspoon kosher salt
1 pound oyster mushrooms, torn into 8 more or less equal pieces
Vegan butter (or vegan mayo)
4 Pão Francês rolls (page 91), Mexican bolillos, Portuguese buns, or 6-inch sections of baguette, split horizontally and warmed
2 plum tomatoes, thinly sliced crosswise
½ cup sliced dill pickles, bread-and-butter pickles, or pickled banana peppers, drained

This dupe of a fried chicken sandwich is made with oyster mushrooms, which have a tender, fleshy texture that makes them a great vegan sub for chicken—they even pull into shreds the same way cooked chicken does. I use potato starch here because it fries up crispy and, more important, seems to stay crispier after frying than 100% flour or cornstarch coatings. It's a damn delicious sandwich, with a lot of heat from both duo jiao and chili oil. In my years as a cook, I've noticed that vegans often have a higher tolerance for spice. If that's not you, just start with less of the chili oil mixture and add it to taste.

Fill a large cast-iron skillet or Dutch oven with neutral oil to a depth of at least 1 inch and heat over medium-high heat to 350°F.

In a large bowl, stir together the chili oil, duo jiao, and five-spice, and set aside.

Set up two shallow bowls near your frying oil. In one, whisk ½ cup of the potato starch with ¼ cup water to create a thick slurry. In the other, mix the remaining ½ cup potato starch with the flour, pepper, and salt. Take a tablespoon of the wet batter and drip it into the dry dredge, mixing briefly with a fork to create some small clumpy bits—these will add extra crunch to the sandwich.

Working quickly, coat the mushrooms in the wet batter, let the excess drip back into the bowl so they are only thinly coated, then toss in the dry mixture to coat. Carefully add the coated mushroom to the hot oil and cook until deeply golden brown, about 4 minutes on each side. Transfer to a paper towel–lined plate to drain.

While the mushrooms are frying, butter the cut sides of the rolls.

While they're still hot, toss the crispy-fried mushrooms in the chili oil mixture, then divide them among the buttered rolls. Garnish with the tomato and pickles and serve immediately.

Snacky Snacks, Bites, and Cravings

Slow, Hot, and Wet:

Soups, Broths, Stews, Braises

When people say they can taste the love someone puts in their food, I believe what they're in fact tasting is time. The process of stewing, braising, and simmering means putting in the necessary work up front and then letting things be and trusting the process. What results are lots of complexity and a richness that is found in the warmest kind of home cooking. To put time into food is to put care into food, and there's not much difference between that and love.

Kung Food

Hong Kong Borscht

Serves 6 to 8

3 tablespoons neutral oil
½ pound beef chuck, cut into 2-inch chunks
1 large white or yellow onion, halved and thinly sliced
3 pods star anise
2 pounds oxtails, sliced into 1-inch pieces by your butcher
1 tablespoon cumin seeds
2 teaspoons freshly ground black pepper, plus more for serving
2 teaspoons ground chipotle chili
2 teaspoons smoked paprika
2 teaspoons garlic powder
3 bay leaves
8 cups beef broth or Superior Stock (page 38), plus extra if needed
3 medium red or purple potatoes, cut into 2-inch chunks
2 cups packed chopped red or green cabbage
3 plum tomatoes, roughly chopped
2 large carrots, sliced ½ inch thick
2 celery stalks, sliced ½ inch thick
1 (6-ounce) can tomato paste
Kosher salt

To the uninitiated, Hong Kong borscht might sound like one of my kooky inventions, but it's actually a cultural icon of Hong Kong. Tart and savory, it's a far cry from the beet-based borscht that most people know, but both originate from Eastern Europe and the cooks who emigrated in the twentieth century due to political unrest.

I like to purchase one large oxtail per person and buy an extra ½- to 1-pound bag of small oxtails from my butcher. While the large oxtails are meaty, the smaller ones are the real source of collagen and flavor. You can pull meat off the bones before serving or leave the larger ones intact. A pressure cooker like the Instant Pot or Ninja Foodi cuts the cooking time by more than half. Serve this as a stew on its own or over rice.

Coat a large stockpot or Dutch oven with oil and heat over medium-high heat. Add the beef in a single layer and cook until deeply browned on all sides, about 10 minutes total. Transfer to a plate and add the onion and star anise to the pot. Cook, stirring occasionally, until the onions are starting to brown, about 8 minutes.

Return the browned beef to the pot along with the oxtails, cumin, pepper, chipotle, paprika, garlic powder, bay leaves, and broth. Raise the heat to high and bring to a boil, then reduce to low, cover, and simmer for 3½ hours (or 45 minutes in a pressure cooker on high); I find that's sufficient to extract most of the flavor and texture from the oxtails. Check occasionally to make sure there is enough liquid to cover the oxtails, adding more broth or water if needed.

Add the potatoes, cabbage, tomatoes, carrots, celery, tomato paste, and a large pinch of salt and stir well. Cover and simmer for another hour. At this point, the potatoes should be very tender and the meat should be falling apart. (If the liquid is too thick, add enough water or broth to reach a hearty stew consistency. If it seems too thin, let it continue cooking, uncovered.) Discard the bay leaves. Taste and season with salt and pepper before serving.

Hong Kong–Style Corn Soup

Serves 2

1 or 2 boneless, skinless chicken
thighs (8 ounces total)
1 tablespoon Shaoxing wine
2 teaspoons light soy sauce
2 teaspoons freshly ground
white pepper
5 teaspoons cornstarch
4 cups fresh corn kernels (from
about 5 ears)
4 cups Herbal Chicken Broth
(page 36) or Superior
Stock (page 38)
1 teaspoon ground turmeric
Kosher salt (optional)
2 large eggs, lightly beaten

There are two soups that define the Hong Kong experience, the first being Hong Kong Borscht (page 99), and the second, this corn soup. It has a silky texture from its cornstarch thickening, and its sweetness is balanced by minced chicken and white pepper. To me, and quite a few generations of Hong Kongers before me, this is classic home cooking. The use of fresh corn versus canned is down to what you can get, what's in season, and what you enjoy (there's a two-Michelin-star restaurant chef in London who adds a foie gras carpaccio to his soup and still insists on using canned corn). Also, because of the gravy-like heartiness of this soup, it's not uncommon for it to be served like a sauce over a bowl of rice. I recommend you try it both ways. This soup is also easily made vegan by omitting the chicken and the egg, using Vegan Broth (page 37), and adding an extra cup of fresh corn kernels (which is how I liked it as a kid).

Mince the chicken thighs and put them in a medium bowl. Add the wine, soy sauce, white pepper, and 2 teaspoons of the cornstarch and mix until the cornstarch is no longer visible. Cover and refrigerate for at least 2 hours or up to 12 hours.

Put 3 cups of the corn kernels in a food processor and purée until very smooth and milky, then transfer to a large saucepan. Add the broth and bring to a boil over high heat, then reduce the heat to maintain a simmer.

Ladle 1 cup of the simmering broth into the bowl with the chicken and stir well, then add the chicken to the saucepan (this prevents the cornstarch in the chicken marinade from clumping). Because the chicken is minced, it will cook through in the short time it takes to finish the soup. Add the remaining 1 cup whole corn kernels to the saucepan.

(recipe continues)

Slow, Hot, and Wet: Soups, Broths, Stews, Braises

In a small bowl, stir together the remaining 3 teaspoons cornstarch, the turmeric, and 2 tablespoons warm tap water until smooth. Stir half this cornstarch slurry into the soup and let it thicken, about a minute; keep stirring as the heat of the soup thickens the slurry. Add more of the cornstarch slurry if you prefer a thicker soup. Taste and add salt, if needed.

Just before serving, with the soup still at a simmer, stir slowly in one direction with a wooden spoon while adding the beaten eggs in a slow, thin stream to make long, dramatic eggy strands. Divide the soup into bowls and serve hot.

102

It might sound odd but try this over rice. I loved that combo when I was little.

Mapo Tofu Kimchi Jjigae

Serves 2

1 tablespoon Szechuan
    peppercorns
1 cup roughly chopped cabbage
    kimchi
1 tablespoon Duo Jiao (page 55)
8 ounces center-cut pork belly,
    skin removed
2 tablespoons gochugaru
    (Korean chili flakes)
5 garlic cloves, grated
½ teaspoon kosher salt
1 tablespoon neutral oil
2 teaspoons
    doubanjiang (Chinese broad
    bean chili paste)
1 (12- to 14-ounce) block
    extra-firm tofu, cut into
    ½-inch cubes
1 white or yellow onion, halved
    and thinly sliced
Steamed rice, for serving
5 scallions, thinly sliced,
    for garnish
3 tablespoons Fragrant Chili Oil
    (page 45), for garnish

I was inspired to make this soup by an online flame war that went on between Chinese and Korean netizens. A tabloid reported that the Chinese had registered an international standard for pao cai, a fermented Chinese vegetable, but failed to report that kimchi was exempt from the categorization, leading some to believe that the Chinese were claiming cultural ownership of kimchi. A fight among those whom I suspect of being perpetually online ensued. It was a crazy claim, and a ridiculous fight, but it didn't stop a decent amount of circulation in Western media, which is how I heard about it. So in what I guess could be solidarity, but also because I was annoyed with the fighting, I decided to blend together two iconic dishes, one Korean and one Chinese.

Now, to make a proper kimchi jjigae, as I learned to do from my friend Eric Kim's fantastic cookbook Korean American, *you need to make the stew with old kimchi. It has the pungency and strength needed to give the stew backbone; using young kimchi will yield a muted taste. You can purchase aged kimchi for this purpose at some Korean grocery stores like H Mart, but lacking that, I suspect the fermented funkiness of duo jiao and the intense saltiness of doubanjiang can pick up the slack a little. Doubanjiang is a Chinese broad bean chili paste necessary for mapo tofu and dry pot.*

In a pan or wok, toast the Szechuan peppercorns over medium-high heat until they are aromatic and wisps of smoke start to appear. Remove and let cool before grinding with a mortar and pestle or spice grinder.

In a small bowl, stir together the kimchi and duo jiao.

Cut the pork belly into ½-inch pieces and put them in a medium bowl with the gochugaru, garlic, and salt. Mix to combine.

(recipe continues)

Kung Food

Coat a heavy saucepan or Dutch oven with neutral oil and heat over medium heat. Add the pork belly and cook, stirring occasionally, until browned on all sides, about 10 minutes total. Stir in the ground Szechuan pepper and cook for 1 minute, then add the doubanjiang, the kimchi mixture, and just enough water to cover. Bring to a boil, then cook for 5 minutes.

Reduce the heat to low, add the tofu and onion, and simmer for about 45 minutes, until the pork is very tender. Serve over rice, garnished with scallions and chili oil.

Mapo Tofu Curry

Serves 4

5 tablespoons neutral oil

2 tablespoons Szechuan chili flakes

1 tablespoon Szechuan peppercorns

2 medium yellow onions, chopped

2 tablespoons curry powder

1 tablespoon Cumin-Based Five-Spice Powder (page 60) or garam masala

2 cups Superior Stock (page 38), homemade or store-bought chicken stock, or Vegan Broth (page 37)

½ (6-ounce) can tomato paste

2 teaspoons doubanjiang

1 teaspoon Chinese vinegar

1 teaspoon light soy sauce

2 blocks (12 to 14 ounces each) extra-firm tofu, drained and cut into ½-inch cubes

1 tablespoon Fragrant Chili Oil (page 45)

Kosher salt

Cilantro, for garnish

Steamed rice, for serving

This recipe is one of my favorites. I often find vegan mapo tofu underwhelming because it lacks the balancing richness and fat that come from using ground pork. So here I make an onion-based curry that calls on the Szechuan mapo tofu spices (chili flakes, tingly peppercorns, fragrant chili oil) in combination with curry powder. I find that the depth of an onion-based curry provides the richness that I missed in mapo tofu with meat. This recipe is a plant-based version with substance that I hope is worthy of the title. When you "veganize" a dish, you can't simply remove the parts that keep it from being vegan; you always have to give something back to the recipe. Everything is there for a reason, especially in classic recipes.

Preseason your wok (see page 29), add 2 tablespoons of oil, and heat over medium.

Add the Szechuan chili flakes and Szechuan peppercorns and toast until fragrant and fried, stirring often, about 2 to 3 minutes (they will have a darker appearance once toasted—but they shouldn't be blackened/burned). Use a slotted spoon to remove the chili flakes and peppercorns from the wok and transfer to a cutting board and crush with a knife or use a mortar and pestle to grind into a crispy powder. If you have a mezzaluna, this is the moment you've been waiting for— use it. A small food processor will also work or even a spice grinder (use one with a washable bowl, you won't get this flavor out of a coffee grinder).

Set the powder aside and return the wok to medium heat. Add 1 tablespoon of oil and the onions, stirring often until they become translucent, about 8 minutes, then add in the curry powder and the five-spice and stir-fry until fragrant, about 1 minute. Mix in half of the stock and then transfer to a blender and blitz until smooth (about 2 minutes on medium speed for a high-speed blender).

Clean, dry, and preseason your wok again. Add the remaining 2 tablespoons of oil to the wok at medium heat along with the tomato paste and doubanjiang and fry, stirring often, until the paste becomes uniform and smooth, about 1 minute.

Stir in the rest of the stock to loosen the paste from the pan, then add the blended curry mixture. Bring to a simmer before turning the heat down to medium-low and add the vinegar, soy sauce, and tofu.

Allow to gently simmer for 10 minutes before topping with fragrant chili oil and crispy chili powder to taste. Season with salt and serve garnished with cilantro and over rice.

I came up with this recipe while creating themed curries based on the gyms in Pokemon Sword and Shield . . . this one was for the Fighting-type gym.

Kung Food

Lion's Head Meatball Soup

Serves 4

Meatballs

2 pounds ground pork
1 (12- to 14-ounce) block
  extra-firm tofu, finely
  crumbled with your hands
5 fresh water chestnuts, peeled
  and minced, or canned water
  chestnuts, rinsed, drained,
  and brunoised
1 bunch scallions, white parts
  only, sliced very thin
¼ cup minced napa cabbage
2 thumb-size pieces fresh
  ginger, peeled and grated
4 garlic cloves, grated
2 teaspoons light soy sauce
2 teaspoons dark soy sauce
2 teaspoons Five-Spice
  Powder (page 59), or use
  store-bought
Neutral oil, for frying

Broth

3 quarts Superior Stock
  (page 38)
3 thumb-size pieces fresh
  ginger, unpeeled, thickly
  sliced
3 star anise pods
3 jujubes

This is my take on a very traditional Chinese dish of pork meatballs in a hearty broth. I use tofu in addition to the pork, which makes the meatballs super light and fluffy. The key is to fry them first, then braise them with cabbage until they become melt-in-your-mouth tender. I encourage you to use the Superior Stock here, since the broth is as important as the meatballs. As an alternative, for a less-soupy dish, you can thicken part of the broth with a cornstarch slurry and serve it as a thick sauce over the meatballs.

Make the meatballs: In a large bowl using clean hands, combine the pork, tofu, water chestnuts, scallions, cabbage, ginger, garlic, light soy sauce, dark soy sauce, and five-spice until everything is very well combined.

Fill a wok with oil to a depth of 3 inches and heat over medium-high heat to 350°F.

Form the meat mixture into 12 equal-size balls and then gently, using a ladle, place them into the hot oil and fry until browned. Don't try to cook them all the way through—you just want a firm outer layer for now. Set aside on a paper towel–lined baking sheet to drain.

Make the broth: Once all the meatballs have been browned, carefully drain the oil in the wok, give the wok a rinse with water and wipe, and replace with the stock, adding the ginger, star anise, and jujubes.

Place the meatballs in the broth and bring to a simmer over medium heat, then reduce the heat to maintain a light simmer. Cover and cook for 45 minutes, until the meatballs float to the top and have cooked all the way through (you can slice one in half to make sure). Serve with the broth as a soup.

Spaghetti and Lion's Head Meatballs

You mean to tell me that you're going to make comically, cartoonishly, large meatballs and not put one on a plate of spaghetti?

Serves 4

Lion's Head Meatballs (see page 111), without
    their broth
1 (16-ounce) can whole peeled San Marzano
    tomatoes
2 tablespoons olive oil
7 garlic cloves, thinly sliced
1 teaspoon ground cumin
1 teaspoon fresh oregano leaves, minced
½ teaspoon cayenne pepper or hot chili powder
Kosher salt
3 sprigs basil
12 ounces dried spaghetti

Prepare the meatballs up to the point when they would go into the broth and set aside. Bring a large pot of water to a boil for the pasta.

Empty the can of tomatoes into a large bowl and crush them well with your hands, then fill the can with water and add that to the bowl as well; set aside.

In a very large sauté pan, heat the olive oil over medium heat. Add the garlic and cumin, let them sizzle for 30 seconds, until fragrant, then add the tomato mixture, oregano, and cayenne and cook for about 5 minutes, until the tomatoes start to break down and the sauce becomes a uniform texture. Taste and season with salt.

Add the meatballs to the sauce and cook, stirring occasionally, for 10 minutes, or until cooked through. In the last few minutes, tear the basil leaves and add them to the pan.

As the sauce cooks, cook the pasta in the boiling water until al dente according to the package directions. Drain the pasta and add it to the pan with the sauce. Use tongs to toss gently, letting the pasta absorb the sauce for about a minute. Serve immediately.

Slow, Hot, and Wet: Soups, Broths, Stews, Braises

Kung Food

White Wood Ear Mushroom and Pear Soup

Serves 4

1 ounce white wood ear mushroom (aka snow fungus)

2 thumb-size pieces fresh ginger, peeled and thinly sliced

1 tablespoon fennel seeds

4 jujubes

2 cinnamon sticks

1 green or black cardamom pod, crushed, seeds removed, and pod discarded

2 Yali or Bosc pears, peeled, halved, and cored

¼ cup goji berries

¼ cup rock sugar or 2 tablespoons honey, plus more (or to taste)

This is actually a traditional Chinese soup, served on its own as a tonic, or as an after-dinner dessert. White wood ear mushroom, a white version of the more common brown variety, is a tasteless tree fungus with a jellylike texture that plays an important role in Chinese medicine. Easily found in Chinese groceries, it's considered a cooling ingredient that fights inflammation, promotes energy, and reduces cough, among other benefits. Pear is also a cooling ingredient; here it's coupled with the warming spices of cinnamon, cardamom, and ginger. Hot or chilled, this tonic is perfectly balanced and appropriate for any time of year.

Put the mushroom in a large bowl and cover with plenty of water. Set aside to soak at room temperature overnight.

The next day, drain the mushroom, then cut off and discard the dark, tough bases. Cut the soaked mushroom into 4 equal quarters and put them in a large saucepan. Add 8 cups water, the ginger, fennel, jujubes, cinnamon, and cardamom. Bring to a boil over high heat, then reduce the heat to low and add the pear halves. Simmer for 30 minutes, then add the goji berries and simmer for 15 minutes more to soften the goji berries and ensure the pears are completely tender. Before serving, taste and add rock sugar or honey; the amount is up to you (I like just enough to bring out the flavor of the other ingredients without it being sugary sweet). Divide the broth among four bowls, adding one pear half and one mushroom piece to each. Leave the spices in the soup, since they look nice and some people like nibbling on the spices, eating the goji berries, etc. Serve hot.

Dried Mushroom and Kabocha Broth

Serves 4 to 6

1 (2- to 3-pound) kabocha squash, halved, seeded, and roughly chopped

1 ounce dried sliced or whole shiitake mushrooms

1 ounce dried porcini mushrooms

2 medium onions, roughly chopped

6 scallions, roughly chopped

3 thumb-size pieces fresh ginger, peeled and thinly sliced

1 finger-size piece fresh or dried turmeric root (if dried, give it a pound in the mortar before using)

1 tablespoon fennel seeds

1 teaspoon whole black peppercorns

3 star anise pods

2 tablespoons red miso paste

Kosher salt (optional)

Two of my favorite fall flavors come together in this rich broth. The squash lends its sweet and creamy nature, while using two types of dried mushrooms gives incredible depth (dried shiitakes are sold both sliced and whole). You can tie the mushrooms in cheesecloth—after they infuse the soup, they'll be soft enough to chop up and add to a pot of congee (but still would be a little tough to eat whole). You can even pick out the squash to eat on its own. No need to peel the kabocha, as its skin is both edible and full of fiber.

In a large saucepan, combine 12 cups water, the squash, shiitake and porcini mushrooms, onions, scallions, ginger, turmeric, fennel, peppercorns, and star anise. Bring to a boil over high heat, then reduce the heat to medium-low, cover, and simmer for 1 hour. Stir in the miso and cook for another 5 minutes. Taste and add salt, if desired.

Strain, discarding the solids (some of the squash will have dissolved into the broth), and serve hot. To make in advance, let cool, then store in a tightly covered container in the fridge for up to a week. Reheat before serving.

Winter Breakfast Broths

Broths can play several roles in a meal. Served at the beginning, they prime the palate, setting the tone for what's to come. Offered in the middle, they act as an interlude, and at the end, they help the body digest. I have a special place in my heart for sipping broth in the morning, as it has the ability to gently warm my body from within, activating it with spices and herbs. This, along with the cold Detroit winter air, inspired me to ask the question "Why don't I drink broth in the morning?" My parents do—they have a light broth along with a light breakfast, and they don't even live somewhere cold.

It's so cold in the D. And in my apartment, where we lacked a proper finished ceiling and any kind of insulation, we would find ourselves waking up to a bedroom that was sub 50°F on the coldest days, even with the heat turned on. I got into the habit of making soups to drink in the morning (nothing too heavy or hearty, because who wants to feel weighed down before work?) to sip from a mug or bowl. When I started sharing videos of myself making these on TikTok, lots of people acted like it was some kind of revelation, and it led to one of my first major viral moments. I was just trying to stay warm. I still make these in my new (much warmer) home. There's something that's really nice about reheating a delicate broth in the morning and enjoying it throughout a winter day.

Note: When we served guests a soup course at my studio kitchen, we would pour it into their bowls straight out of large water kettles (like Brits use for tea) reserved exclusively for soup. This made sure that every guest got piping-hot soup (and also made it less likely that any soup would spill as it got to them), and it's a trick I still use in my own home. Keep a kettle of broth warm during your work-from-home days. Soup kettles: Tell your friends. Tell your auntie.

Coffee and Mushroom Broth

Serves 4 to 6

½ cup dried porcini mushrooms
1 cup dried sliced or whole
shiitake mushrooms
1 cup store-bought roasted
barley or Korean barley tea
1 tablespoon mushroom powder
1 teaspoon fennel seeds
½ teaspoon allspice berries
2 star anise pods
1 teaspoon kosher salt
Cold-brew coffee concentrate,
at room temperature, as
needed
Steamed oat milk or other
nondairy milk (optional)
1 dried morel mushroom
(optional)

I came up with this broth completely by accident at a restaurant where I worked. I made a vegan mushroom broth for my chef and still had some of its flavor on my palate as I took a swig of my cold brew and realized they tasted quite nice together. Here the coffee plays more of a background role. The milk is purely optional, but it turns this into something between a cream of mushroom broth and a latte with dried morel grated on top for drama.

In a large saucepan, combine 12 cups water, the porcini and shiitake mushrooms, barley, mushroom powder, fennel, allspice, star anise, and salt. Bring to a boil over high heat, then reduce the heat to low and simmer, uncovered, for 45 minutes.

Strain the broth (discard the solids) and serve hot. To serve, pour into large coffee mugs and add 2 tablespoons cold-brew concentrate per mugful. Add steamed milk and/or milk foam, using a Microplane, grate the morel over the top as you would chocolate or nutmeg, if desired. To make in advance, let cool, then store in a tightly covered container in the fridge for up to a week. Reheat before serving.

Roasted barley is available in most Asian groceries. It's steeped on its own as a tea, but I find it gives a deep, nutty low note to certain broths and soups.

Slow, Hot, and Wet: Soups, Broths, Stews, Braises

Chinese Ham and
Melon Broth

Makes about 12 cups

2 overly ripe cantaloupes (see Note)

4 ounces Xi Shàng Xi cured ham (or Jinhua ham, if you can source it), or another salt-cured ham (see Note)

Kosher salt and/or honey

It's Saturday morning at the kitchen where I used to work and one of our farmers comes in with a crate of overripe melons. "They were good a couple of days ago, but I can't sell them now, and I don't want to bring them back, so here." He drops them off and then goes to the distillery next door. He'll come back for the crate tomorrow. Looking at the melons, I can see that they're getting a touch moldy at the ends. I can cut those parts off, but what am I going to do with 15 pounds of melon that need to be used today? At my disposal I have an old 1970s Garland stove (we call her Judy) that has two heat settings—off and hell—as well as a stockpot. I did happen to purchase a box of Chinese ham that my guy was trying to get rid of . . . I guess I could try making a soup?

Cut the cantaloupes in half, remove the seeds, and scoop all the flesh into a large saucepan. Add the ham and 16 cups water and bring to a boil over high heat. Reduce the heat to medium-low and simmer, uncovered, for 1 hour, then taste—it should be both sweet and salty, with the melon and ham flavors both prominent. If the taste isn't strong enough for you at this stage, cook longer to reduce it down more. Add salt and/or honey to find the perfect sweet-and-salty balance for you (depending on the type of ham, it might already be salty or sweet enough).

Strain the broth, reserving the ham for another use (mince it for dumpling fillings, dice it for fried rice, or matchstick it to top noodles), and discard any cantaloupe that hasn't dissolved into the broth. Serve hot. To make in advance, let cool, then store in a tightly covered container in the fridge for up to a week. Reheat before serving.

Note on the melons: They should be so ripe that they threaten to ferment. You should almost be able to squeeze the melon in half—it should be that ripe. If you walk into the room and you don't immediately smell musky melon, your melon is not yet ready. Once it's ripe enough, cut the mold off the outer rind (if there is any) and halve the melon—the seeds should nearly fall out on their own, and the flesh should be so soft that if you choose to, you can scoop it out effortlessly using your hand.

Note on the ham: Western hams do not taste the same as dense, salty Chinese hams. You'll be missing out on 80 percent of the character if you try this with a regular ham. Jinhua ham, my preferred type, isn't available in the United States, but an American-made equivalent by Xi Shàng Xi brand can be found at almost all Chinese grocery stores, as well as online. The ham is usually packaged in pairs of slices, and you need only one slice for every two melons.

The great thing about dumplings is that they exist in some way, shape, or form in almost all culinary cultures. Whether the skills traveled across continents over centuries or were developed independently over time in cultural vacuums, it seems like if a group of people managed to learn to cook, eventually their culinary journey led them to dumplings.

Unless you're making a specialized type of dumpling (such as soup dumplings) or a style that has more intricate pleats and requires a more malleable homemade wrapper as a result, store-bought wrappers (I like the Twin Marquis brand) can produce very good results.

Noodles + Dumplings

Similarly, while making your own noodles is great and gives you an appreciation of the craft, there are only so many hours in the day, and I'd rather you focus on the broths and sauces and living your life rather than stressing over the alkalinity of a dough. I almost always use someone else's noodles (heh) when cooking for myself, so why would it be different for anyone else? Finally, nothing is stopping you from replacing soup noodles with boiled wontons or dumplings. A huge bowl of wontons in a broth topped with chili oil and a mountain of scallions is an elite combination. One of my favorite easy meals at home is frozen dumplings treated as you would any kind of dried pasta, just boiling them and adding them to literally any kind of sauce—chili oil, pesto, a TikTok viral vodka sauce, even Japanese instant curry. It's easy enough to throw together after a long day, and if you manage to make them after a long night out you're everyone's hero.

Kung Food

Ginger Scallion Noodles

Serves 2

8 ounces noodles

2 tablespoons Ginger Scallion Oil (page 53), raw or cooked, plus more as desired

Optional toppings: steamed vegetables, poached or soft-boiled egg, duo jiao, kecap manis, chili crisp

This is a showcase for ginger scallion oil, so I prefer to limit my toppings to gently flavored ones like steamed vegetables and eggs, with dabs of kecap manis for sweetness or duo jiao for heat. I particularly like a thick and chewy noodle for this, like the belt-shaped noodles used for the Xi'an dish biang biang mian. Look for any broad, flat, wheat-based noodle.

Cook the noodles according to the package directions and drain well. Stir in the ginger scallion oil and divide among shallow serving bowls. Serve additional oil alongside, as well as any of the suggested toppings.

The first time I made this for my boyfriend, he gripped the table in amazement. People who react to eating food like this is a weakness for any cook.

Cold Chili Oil Noodles

Serves 2

8 ounces noodles
2 tablespoons Fragrant Chili
    Oil (page 45) or Chorizo
    Chili Oil (page 47)
1 teaspoon Zhenjiang black
    vinegar
1 teaspoon light soy sauce
¼ cup thinly sliced scallions
1 tablespoon toasted hulled
    sesame seeds

Optional toppings: pickled
    vegetables, chopped roasted
    peanuts, poached egg, gan
    lan cai (Chinese preserved
    olive vegetable), slivered
    cucumber, kohlrabi, bok choy

I don't remember when I first started eating cold noodles regularly, but before we got air-conditioning, they were one of my favorite ways to keep cool in the kitchen. Chilling the noodles after cooking also gives them a delightfully bouncy bite. I prefer Shanxi planed noodles, which are not as broad as those I used in the ginger scallion noodles but still thick and provide a satisfying chew. You can also use spaghetti-like Shanghai-style noodles for this.

Cook the noodles according to the package directions and drain well. Fill a large bowl with ice and water and place the noodles in the ice bath to fully cool, then drain well again.

Transfer the noodles to a large bowl and add the chili oil, vinegar, and soy sauce. Add the scallions and sesame seeds and use two spoons to toss and distribute the ingredients evenly. Serve with additional toppings alongside.

Noodles + Dumplings

Hot Chili Oil Noodles

Serves 2

8 ounces noodles

3 cups Herbal Chicken Broth
(page 36), Superior Stock
(page 38), or Vegan Broth
(page 37)

¼ cup Fragrant Chili Oil
(page 45)

Optional toppings: steamed
bok choy, sautéed or grilled
tofu, fried egg, Chinese
pickled vegetables, shredded
chicken, chorizo crisps (left
over from making Chorizo
Chili Oil, page 47), peanuts,
sesame seeds, fresh cilantro

Besides the temperature difference compared with Cold Chili Oil Noodles (page 126), these are also served in a broth, as a kind of noodle/soup hybrid. The chili oil floats to the top, giving a glistening contrast of bright red over the broth, and it sticks to the noodles as you raise them out of your bowl. It lends itself to being loaded up with lots of fixings such as pickles, eggs, meats, steamed vegetables, grilled tofu, and more. Here the Shanghai-style or broad wonton noodle would work well.

Cook the noodles according to the package directions and drain well. In a separate pot, bring the broth to a boil, then turn off the heat.

Divide the noodles among serving bowls and stir some chili oil into each, then pour some hot broth over the top. Add toppings to taste and serve.

The Limitless
Noodle Bowl

The noodle recipes here are meant to be suggestions, not rules. I'm always changing the noodle type and quantity as well as the accompanying sauces and toppings based on my mood, what looks good in the market, or whatever is lying around the kitchen at the time.

If you're cooking for a group, set out several sauces and toppings next to preportioned bowls of noodles. You can include condiments like soy sauce, chili oil, kecap manis, sambal, doubanjiang, and gochujang; vegetable seasonings like minced raw garlic, minced ginger, fried shallots, and Chinese preserved olive vegetable; and heartier toppings like cooked greens and vegetables, shredded cooked chicken, and stir-fried tofu. Keep a pot of broth on a rolling boil if you're doing this so it reheats the noodles as you ladle some on.

Eat your noodles out of comically large bowls because the tall rims stop the broth from splashing onto your shirt.

130

Noodles for Breakfast

Serves 1

1½ cups broth of some kind (like the ones on pages 36 to 38), or 2 tablespoons mentsuyu with a little hot water (whatever you have time for)

1 or 2 slices thick-cut bacon, fried until crispy, then crumbled (optional)

1 tablespoon unsalted butter

1 (3-ounce) bundle somen noodles

1 large egg

Kosher salt

1 scallion, halved lengthwise and cut crosswise into ½-inch lengths

Apparently, this is a concept so alien to people that a very casual and unassuming TikTok about it garnered over 14 million views and countless Instagram tags from people giving it a try. Such a basic thing: some broth or a few splashes of mentsuyu (bottled Japanese noodle soup base), somen noodles (because of their barely-a-minute cooking time), a fried egg, and scallions. (A little crispy-fried bacon is a nice topping, too.) The real beauty in this is how quickly it takes once you get the motions down.

Bring some water to a boil for the noodles. Have the broth simmering in a separate small pot. If you're including bacon, put it in your serving bowl.

When the water is boiling, melt the butter in a small nonstick pan over medium heat. Add the noodles to the boiling water (cook according to package instructions) and then crack the egg into the buttered pan and cook as desired (I do over-easy); the noodles and egg should be done around the same time. Drain the noodles and add them to your serving bowl, then pour in the broth; the noodles and broth will heat the bacon through. Lightly salt the egg and add it to the bowl, along with the butter from the pan. Top with the scallions.

131

Jerk Chow Mein

Serves 4

2 bunches scallions, roughly
chopped
2 garlic cloves, peeled
2 Scotch bonnet or habanero
peppers, stemmed and
seeded (use gloves or be very
careful not to touch your eyes
after handling!)
1 thumb-size piece fresh ginger,
peeled and roughly chopped
2 tablespoons sweet paprika
1 tablespoon light brown sugar
2 teaspoons freshly ground
allspice
2 teaspoons fresh thyme leaves
2 teaspoons kosher salt
1 teaspoon freshly ground black
pepper
¼ teaspoon ground or freshly
grated nutmeg
8 ounces protein (thinly sliced
pork loin, beef tenderloin,
chicken thigh, or firm tofu)
12 ounces fresh chow mein
noodles (see Note)
Neutral oil
8 ounces sturdy vegetables
(such as cauliflower, broccoli,
baby bok choy, or snow peas),
cut into small pieces

The history of the Chinese diaspora in relation to the Caribbean is an interesting one. In the mid-1850s, thousands of people from China were brought to the British Caribbean to work as indentured laborers (slaves), primarily on the islands of Guyana, Jamaica, and Trinidad, and more arrived in waves over the next two decades. This steady influx led to the development of Caribbean Chinese cuisine, which blends West Indian flavors with the (mainly) Cantonese palate and cooking techniques. Jerk chow mein is one of the staples of this cuisine. If using meat as opposed to tofu, let it marinate in the jerk spice rub for at least 2 hours or up to 24 hours before cooking.

In a food processor, combine the scallions, garlic, Scotch bonnets, ginger, paprika, brown sugar, allspice, thyme, salt, black pepper, and nutmeg and blend to a paste. Set aside. If using meat as opposed to tofu, coat it lightly with about a tablespoon of the jerk sauce and refrigerate for at least 2 hours or up to 24 hours.

Blanch or cook the noodles according to the package directions (see Note); drain and set aside. Coat a wok with neutral oil and heat over medium-high heat. Add the meat or tofu and the vegetables and stir-fry until the vegetables start to char and the meat is almost cooked through, about 3 to 4 minutes, depending on your wok's heat. Add the noodles and the jerk sauce and toss until everything is evenly mixed and coated, and the meat is fully cooked through, about a minute longer. Serve.

Note: Fresh (i.e., not dried) chow mein noodles are generally sold in two forms: steamed or raw. If they say steamed on the package, and/ or have no cooking directions, they just need to be blanched in boiling water for 30 seconds and drained before they're pan-fried in your dish. If the package says raw, then follow the cooking instructions on the package before pan-frying.

133

Noodles + Dumplings

Curry Goat Lo Mein

Serves 4

Goat and marinade

- 1 pound boneless goat stew meat (or lamb), trimmed of fat and cut into 1-inch cubes
- 1 cup fresh lemon juice (from 4 to 5 lemons) or rice wine or coconut vinegar
- 1 tablespoon Cumin-Based Five-Spice Powder (page 60)
- 1 tablespoon ground turmeric
- 2 teaspoons garlic powder
- 2 teaspoons ground black pepper
- 1 teaspoon ground allspice
- 1 teaspoon onion powder
- 1 teaspoon kosher salt
- 1 teaspoon chicken bouillon powder
- 1 yellow onion, diced
- 1 Scotch bonnet or habanero pepper, stemmed, seeded, and minced (use gloves!)
- 1 tablespoon grated fresh ginger
- 1 tablespoon minced garlic (about 3 cloves)
- 2 teaspoons Tomato Soy Sauce (page 52) or light soy sauce
- 2 teaspoons Shaoxing wine
- 1 tablespoon neutral oil
- 1 sprig thyme (preferably lemon thyme), leaves removed from stems

I loved lo mein as a kid and I'm not sure why it took me a while to revisit it as an adult. This recipe is a great use of my cumin-based five-spice powder and its affinity for goat and lamb. Be aware that the goat needs to marinate for at least six hours before browning . . . and I like to let it go even longer—like up to two days—for the deepest flavor.

Marinate the goat: Add the goat meat and lemon juice or vinegar to a large bowl and cover with water. Using your hands, rinse the meat well in the liquid and drain. Return the goat to the bowl, cover with just water, rinse again, and drain well. (If making this with lamb, you can skip the rinsing.)

Pat the meat dry so the seasonings have an easier time adhering. Return the meat to the bowl and toss with the five-spice, turmeric, garlic powder, pepper, allspice, onion powder, salt, and bouillon. Add the onion, Scotch bonnet, ginger, garlic, soy sauce, Shaoxing wine, oil, and thyme and rub into the goat meat. Cover the bowl with plastic and refrigerate for at least 2 hours or up to 2 days (the longer the goat marinates, the more flavor it will have).

Braise the goat: Remove goat from the marinade and pat dry. Set a wok over medium-high heat and add the oil. Once the oil is shimmering, add the five-spice, turmeric, garlic powder, onion powder, allspice, and pepper and cook, stirring often, until the spices start to foam (it should be almost immediately). Add the goat and give it a good sear in the wok until the meat is very nicely coated in the spices, some of it starts to char a bit, and the aromas really start to open up (about 3 minutes).

Add enough stock to just cover the meat and then turn the heat down to medium-low and cook for about 1 hour, until the goat is cooked through and almost at the desired tenderness. After an hour, add the potatoes and carrots and cook for another 20 to 30 minutes until the vegetables become tender. Add salt to taste. (You can keep this

Braising

2 tablespoons neutral oil
2 teaspoons Cumin-Based
  Five-Spice Powder
  (page 60)
2 teaspoons ground turmeric
2 teaspoons garlic powder
2 teaspoons onion powder
1 teaspoon ground allspice
1 teaspoon freshly ground black
  pepper
2 quarts (8 cups) chicken stock
  or beef stock
3 to 4 medium red potatoes,
  quartered
2 carrots, chopped into large
  pieces
Kosher salt

Lo mein

12 ounces lo mein noodles
1 tablespoon cornstarch
Thinly sliced scallions or cilantro
  leaves

hearty gravy up to a few days in the fridge and mix in the noodles later. Curry always tastes better the next day anyway.)

Prepare and finish the lo mein: If the noodles need to be parboiled before stir-frying, do so now (check the package).

Mix the cornstarch with ¼ cup water to create a slurry. Just before serving, turn the heat up under the goat until the liquid comes to a low boil, then add in a little of the cornstarch slurry and stir until the desired gravy thickness has been reached (I like my gravy to be pretty substantial but not overly heavy or gelled).

Add the noodles and scrape the bottom of the wok to bring the contents over the noodles, constantly mixing until the noodles are well coated and the goat meat and vegetables are evenly dispersed. Garnish with scallions or cilantro and serve.

Chao Nian Gao

Serves 2

12 ounces sliced rice cakes, thawed, if frozen

4 dried shiitake mushrooms

8 ounces pork loin or boneless, skinless chicken thighs, thinly sliced

3 tablespoons light soy sauce

2 tablespoons Shaoxing wine

1 teaspoon toasted sesame oil

½ teaspoon freshly ground white pepper

2 tablespoons oyster sauce

1 tablespoon dark soy sauce

2 teaspoons hoisin sauce

1 teaspoon Zhenjiang black vinegar

1 teaspoon cornstarch

2 tablespoons neutral oil

3 garlic cloves, grated

2 teaspoons grated fresh ginger

3 heads baby bok choy, leaves separated (with white ribs)

This is my version of Shanghainese stir-fried rice cakes. They're often eaten during the New Year because the name of the dish also sounds like "a year of growth." Oddly, there are two Chinese dishes with the name nian gao. The Hong Kong version is a dessert while the Shanghainese version (this one) is a savory stir-fried dish (which is why it's called chao nian gao, chao=stir-fried). The rice cakes in this dish are shaped like slanted coins and can be found dried and refrigerated. Korean rice cakes are usually cylindrical, but there are coin-shaped ones as well (specifically the ones used for tteokguk), which are easy to find in Korean groceries and online. Though their textures differ slightly, you can use either Chinese or Korean rice cakes for this recipe, and they can be frozen, refrigerated, or dried.

Soak the rice cake in cold water for two hours or overnight in the refrigerator.

Put the dried shiitakes in a small bowl with ½ cup water and soak at room temperature overnight.

When ready to cook, remove the mushrooms from the water and set aside; strain the soaking liquid and set it aside separately. Remove and discard any tough stems from the mushrooms and slice them ½ inch thick.

In a small bowl, combine the meat with 1 tablespoon of the light soy sauce, the wine, sesame oil, and white pepper and toss to coat. Marinate in the refrigerator for 1 hour.

(recipe continues)

In another bowl, mix the remaining 2 tablespoons light soy sauce, the oyster sauce, dark soy sauce, hoisin, and vinegar. Whisk in the cornstarch until it dissolves, then set aside.

Heat a wok over medium heat until hot, then add 1 tablespoon of the oil, the garlic, and the ginger and stir-fry just until their aromas release, about 30 seconds. Add the meat with its marinade and cook, stirring frequently, until much of the pink has been cooked out, for 3 to 4 minutes. Add the mushrooms and stir for 20 seconds. Add the bok choy and stir again for 20 seconds. Scrape the ingredients from the wok into a medium bowl.

Place the wok back over high heat and add the remaining 1 tablespoon oil. Add the rice cakes and cook until lightly browned, about 1 to 2 minutes. Pour in the reserved mushroom soaking water and cover the wok; cook for 2 minutes to steam the rice cakes. Taste one rice cake for texture; some brands take longer to cook, but they should be bouncy and tender. When the rice cakes are ready, return the meat mixture to the wok, along with the sauce mixture. Stir to quickly and fully incorporate, then cook until the sauce thickens and the rice cakes are brown and glossy, about 2 minutes. Transfer to a medium bowl and serve immediately.

Dan Dan Noodles with 蛋
(Dan Dan Noodles with Egg)

Serves 4

Sauce

⅓ cup Fragrant Chili Oil (page 45)
2 tablespoons roasted sesame paste or tahini
2 tablespoons light soy sauce
2 teaspoons sugar
1 teaspoon Five-Spice Powder (page 59), or use store-bought
3 garlic cloves, grated

Noodles

8 ounces Shanghai-stye noodles or other thin wheat noodles
1 bunch greens, such as bok choy, yu choy, or Broccolini (about 6 ounces), roughly chopped

Note: Have all your ingredients measured and ready, as each part of this recipe comes together quickly.

So there I was, working my shift at Noodle & Congee Corner at the Grand Lisboa hotel and casino in Macau, when I saw my 師/师 (chef-teacher) bring out, of all things, a few jars of Jif peanut butter. I was very confused and could think of only one dish we had on the menu that could possibly have any use for such a thing. So, in my terrible Chinese, I muttered, "Is . . . is that for . . . the dan dan noodles?"

My 師/师 looked at me, smirked, and said, "Oh, you're clever," and then she emptied the peanut butter into a bowl of soy sauce and chili oil. "We like using this because the sweetness removes the step of adding sugar to balance out the sauce. It's more efficient this way, and it's generally a better quality product." Even then, while surrounded by state-of-the-art Chinese induction restaurant equipment (still light-years ahead of anything we have in the US even as I write this in 2023), the assumption that some American-made things are better in quality still held.

"Also," the porpor (granny) making the fresh wontons next to me chimed in, as she grabbed the now empty jar of Jif, "these containers last forever once you wash them."

I don't make my dan dan noodles with Jif as they did there. But it was an important lesson to me in putting recipes on pedestals. Sometimes, being clever and pragmatic is the most "authentic" way to make anything.

Make the sauce: In a small bowl, mix together the chili oil, sesame paste, light soy sauce, sugar, and five-spice. Set aside, with the three grated garlic cloves in a separate dish.

Make the noodles: Fill a large pot with water and bring to a boil over high heat. Add the noodles and cook according to the package

(recipe and ingredients continue)

142

Meat

1 tablespoon hoisin sauce

1 tablespoon oyster sauce

2 teaspoons dark soy sauce

¼ teaspoon Five-Spice Powder (page 59), or use store-bought

2 tablespoons neutral oil

1 tablespoon chopped dried Szechuan chilies or other hot red chilies (optional)

3 garlic cloves, grated

4 ounces ground pork

3 tablespoons ya cai (preserved mustard greens; see Note)

¼ cup Shaoxing wine

To finish

2 poached eggs (or sous vide, see page 62; optional)

2 tablespoons chopped unsalted roasted peanuts

2 scallions, thinly sliced

¼ teaspoon Basic Szechuan Peppercorn Oil (page 46; optional), as a finishing oil

directions, then, about 30 seconds before the noodles are done, add the greens—they need only 30 seconds to soften and turn bright green. Drain, reserving ¼ cup of the cooking water.

Cook the meat: In a small bowl, mix together the hoisin, oyster sauce, dark soy sauce, and five-spice.

Set a wok over high heat and add the oil and the dried chilies (if using). Once hot, add the garlic and cook, stirring, about 30 seconds, until it starts to turn golden, then add the ground pork. Stir-fry until the pork is almost cooked (with just a trace of pink remaining), then add the ya cai and stir to heat through. Add the wine and stir, scraping up any stuck bits from the bottom and sides of the wok. When the wine has almost evaporated, mix in the hoisin mixture, then transfer everything to a bowl. Cover the bowl to keep warm until serving.

Finish the sauce: Reduce the heat under the wok to low, add the garlic (no need to clean the wok first), and stir-fry until it starts to turn golden; this will happen quickly. Add the chili oil mixture and the reserved ¼ cup noodle cooking water. Stir to combine and let the mixture come to a simmer; it's ready once it starts to bubble.

To serve, divide the noodles and greens between four bowls. Top with the sauce, then the pork mixture, then the eggs, if desired. Garnish with the peanuts and scallions, and finish with the Szechuan peppercorn oil, if you like.

Note: Ya cai (Chinese pickled mustard greens) are dried and fermented, giving them an intensity of flavor that is a hallmark of many Szechuan dishes. Ya cai's popularity among Chinese pickles means it's readily available in Chinese groceries. They usually come in small, sealed pouches and are shelf stable before opening.

143

Dumplings, Wontons, Rangoons, and Dim Sims

I've never been completely sure what the difference is between dumplings and wontons. I always assumed it was that wontons are made with a hot water dough, producing a thinner, more delicate wrapper, while dumpling wrappers are made with cold water, which produces a thicker, more structured dough. There don't seem to be any hard-and-fast rules, though. Rangoons, meanwhile, are a deep-fried later invention, and dim sims are an Aussie specialty. Here we're keeping things simple and going with manufactured wrappers, which seem to follow the rule that square wrappers are for wontons and round ones are for dumplings.

Steaming

Steaming is a healthy way to cook dumplings that is gentle enough to cook the dumplings without jostling them, which allows them to keep their shape. Because it's such a gentle cooking method, the shape of the dumpling holds together, which is ideal if you're performing more delicate and intricate folds. Also, everything looks good served in a steamer basket.

To steam: Set your steamer basket(s) in a wok or skillet that is at least 1 to 2 inches larger than the steamer. Add enough water to come up just to the bottom of the steamer without touching it. Remove the steamer and bring the water to a boil over high heat. Meanwhile, line the bottom of the steamer with a single layer of cabbage leaves, then a piece of parchment paper (cut to fit) or a nonstick liner; do the same for each subsequent layer of steamer you place on top of the first. Place the dumplings in the lined steamer in a single layer, not touching, and cover with the lid. When the water is boiling, place the steamer basket over the wok or skillet. Steam until the filling is cooked through, usually 8 to 10 minutes (refer to the instructions in the recipe for specific cooking times).

Note: Woks are great for steaming because of the conical shape; you'll always be able to fit a steamer basket in one wok as opposed to finding a saucepan or pot that will fit perfectly. Also, any water that drips from the steamer basket will fall back into a wok versus down the sides of a straight sided pot.

Boiling

Boiling dumplings is great if you're serving a lot of people—unlike steaming, you can boil a whole bunch at once, in one pot or in many. This is the way to go when you're cooking dumplings for a party or other large group. Because the cooking method is somewhat aggressive, it's possible that delicate folds may fall apart as they cook, so reserve this for dumplings with thicker wrappers and more basic folds. The texture and flavor of the finished dumplings is similar to steaming. Try to be as gentle as you can; bring the frozen dumplings to a boil first but then reduce the pot to a gentle simmer to minimize too much jostling in the pot.

To boil: Bring a large pot of lightly salted water to a boil over high heat. Add as many dumplings as will fit while still allowing water to circulate around each one and stir gently so they don't stick together. Cook at a gentle boil (you may want to reduce the heat from high to medium-high) until the filling is cooked through, about 6 to 8 minutes, depending on size.

Pan-Frying

Pan-frying dumplings involves searing them on one side in a hot skillet until browned on the bottom, then adding water and covering the pan to steam the dumplings the rest of the way through. Pan-fried dumplings are for fans of crispy bottoms.

To pan-fry: Coat the bottom of a nonstick pan with neutral oil and heat over medium heat. Add enough dumplings to fill the pan in a single layer without touching and cook, until golden brown on the bottom, about 3 minutes (do not move them). Add enough water to cover the entire bottom of the pan (½ to 1 cup), then cover and cook until the filling is cooked through, about 6 to 8 minutes, checking halfway to make sure there is enough water to finish steaming. Uncover the pan and cook off any remaining water before removing the dumplings.

Deep-Frying

If you crave crunchy, golden-brown-all-over dumplings, this is the way to go. Also, frying dumplings is pretty gentle on the cooking oil (as opposed to frying fish or heavily breaded chicken), so it can be strained and reused quite a few times before it needs to be discarded. Make a large batch of these and keep them warm in the oven for parties.

To deep-fry: Fill a wok or pot with neutral oil to a depth of at least 3 inches. Heat the oil over medium-high heat to 350°F. Add the dumplings to the hot oil in batches—you don't want to overcrowd the dumplings or they won't fry properly. Fry until the wrappers are deep golden brown, about 3 minutes, using tongs or a slotted spoon to turn the dumplings occasionally so all sides become browned. Use a slotted spoon or spider to transfer the fried dumplings to a paper towel–lined plate or baking sheet to drain while you fry the next batch. Serve hot.

Note: Frozen dumplings can be cooked via any of these methods without thawing first; they might just need an extra minute or two of cooking time.

Dumpling Dipping Sauce

This is my favorite dipping sauce and it literally takes ten seconds to put together.

Makes ¼ cup

2 tablespoons Fragrant Chili Oil (page 45), or store-bought chili oil
2 tablespoons light soy sauce
1 large garlic clove, smashed

Stir the chili oil, soy sauce, and garlic together in a small bowl. Remove the garlic clove before serving, or don't.

Other things to eat with dumplings: Store-bought chili crisp, ginger scallion oil, kecap manis, duo jiao, black or red vinegar.

Noodles + Dumplings

Kung Food

Pork and Chive Dumplings

Makes 12 dumplings

1 teaspoon cornstarch
4 ounces ground pork
1 cup minced fresh Chinese
    chives (also called nira green
    or garlic chives)
1 tablespoon Shaoxing wine
1 teaspoon light soy sauce
1 teaspoon dark soy sauce
12 dumpling wrappers, circular
    or square
Dumpling Dipping Sauce
    (page 146), for serving

Think of this as a good starter recipe when you're learning how to make dumplings, and especially how to fold them. Because there are no hard or sharp ingredients (like carrots or cabbage), they're easy to fold without ripping the wrapper. This is probably the most common dumpling filling, both in China and in the US, and it is equally good for any cooking method.

In a large bowl, mix the cornstarch with 2 teaspoons cool tap water until smooth. Add the pork, chives, wine, and light and dark soy sauces and mix until uniform in texture.

Set a small bowl of water on your work surface. Place the dumpling wrappers on a cutting board and use a small spoon to add about 2 teaspoons of the filling to the center of each wrapper.

Store-bought wrappers come in a few varieties, including Hong Kong–style ones made yellow by the addition of an alkaline solution (or food coloring) to the dough, green ones made using spinach, and very large squares and rectangles for egg rolls. But the basic ones you need are the palm-size circles (usually labeled "dumpling wrapper") and squares (usually "wonton wrapper"). When making dumplings, the number you end up with will depend on how much filling you include in each one. It's always a good idea to have extra wrappers on hand, too, as sometimes they get stuck together or torn.

This is the simplest way to fold: Dip a finger into the water and moisten the edges of the bottom half of the wrapper, then fold the top over the bottom, enclosing the filling while pushing out any trapped air. Press on the edges to seal. You can moisten and pleat the sealed edges, if desired. Repeat with the remaining wrappers.

Proceed to steam, boil, pan-fry, or deep-fry the dumplings following the instructions on pages 144 through 146. Serve with dipping sauce on the side.

149

Fried Lamb Curry Wontons

Makes 12 wontons

1 teaspoon cornstarch
4 ounces ground lamb
¼ cup cream cheese
1 tablespoon Shaoxing wine
1 tablespoon Muchi curry
   powder or vindaloo curry
   powder
1 teaspoon light soy sauce
1 teaspoon dark soy sauce
12 thin square wonton wrappers
Dumpling Dipping Sauce
   (page 146), for serving

The spices in store-bought curry powder are almost always raw and need to have their flavor brought out by cooking in oil or ghee before the curry powder is incorporated into the dish. Here, because the raw powder is added to the filling, deep-frying is the best cooking method, as the high heat of the oil brings out the best flavor of the curry powder.

In a large bowl, mix the cornstarch with 2 teaspoons cool tap water until smooth. Add the lamb, cream cheese, wine, curry powder, and soy sauces and mix with clean hands until uniform in texture.

Set a small bowl of water on your work surface. Place the wonton wrappers on a cutting board and use a small spoon to add about 2 teaspoons of the filling to the center of each wrapper.

This is the simplest way to fold: Dip a finger into the water and moisten the edges of the bottom half of the wrapper, then fold the top over the bottom, enclosing the filling while pushing out any trapped air. Press on the edges to seal. You can moisten and pleat the sealed edges, if desired. Repeat with the remaining wrappers.

Deep-fry the wontons following the instructions on page 146. Serve with dipping sauce on the side.

Chicken and Cabbage Dumplings

Makes 12 dumplings

2 teaspoons cornstarch
4 ounces ground chicken
1 cup minced napa cabbage
3 scallions, very thinly sliced
1 tablespoon grated fresh ginger
1 teaspoon light soy sauce
1 teaspoon kosher salt
1 teaspoon freshly ground white
    pepper
1 teaspoon freshly ground black
    pepper
2 teaspoons chicken bouillon
    powder
12 dumpling wrappers, circular
    or square
Dumpling Dipping Sauce
    (page 146), for serving

Ground chicken—ground white meat poultry in general—has a much more delicate structure than other ground meats. Because of this it can break down more easily than other ground meats so adding too much liquid will create an unworkable filling that's impossible to fold into a wrapper. To combat this, use a little extra cornstarch, and keep the liquid seasonings to a minimum. This filling can be boiled, steamed, and pleasantly fried, and goes very well with a chunky ginger scallion oil.

In a large bowl, mix the cornstarch with 2 teaspoons cool tap water until smooth. Add the chicken, cabbage, scallions, ginger, soy sauce, salt, white and black pepper, and bouillon and mix with clean hands until uniform in texture.

Set a small bowl of water on your work surface. Place the dumpling wrappers on a cutting board and use a small spoon to add about 2 teaspoons of the filling to the center of each wrapper.

This is the simplest way to fold: Dip a finger into the water and moisten the edges of the bottom half of the wrapper, then fold the top over the bottom, enclosing the filling while pushing out any trapped air. Press on the edges to seal. You can moisten and pleat the sealed edges, if desired. Repeat with the remaining wrappers.

Proceed to steam, boil, pan-fry, or deep-fry the dumplings following the instructions on pages 144 through 146. Serve with dipping sauce on the side.

151

Vegetable and Tofu Dumplings

Makes 24 dumplings

2 teaspoons cornstarch

½ (14-ounce) block extra-firm tofu, drained and crumbled as finely as possible

1 large carrot, grated

1 small red or yellow bell pepper, minced as finely as possible

3 button or cremini mushrooms, stemmed and minced as finely as possible

1 tablespoon grated fresh ginger

2 garlic cloves, grated

2 teaspoons light soy sauce

1 teaspoon MSG or mushroom bouillon powder (see page 25)

1 teaspoon toasted sesame oil

24 dumpling wrappers, circular or square

Dumpling Dipping Sauce (page 146), black vinegar, or chili crisp, for serving

This vegan filling is a looser mixture that can be a little more challenging to fold into a wrapper, so use the folding technique you're most comfortable with. If you're a fan of pickled and pungent flavors, you can add 1 tablespoon olive vegetable, ya cai, ½ teaspoon doubanjiang (spicy), or ½ cup of drained and minced kimchi. You can pan-fry these or boil them in vegan broth to make a hearty vegan noodle soup (see opposite page).

In a large bowl, mix the cornstarch with 2 teaspoons cool tap water until smooth. Add the tofu, carrot, bell pepper, mushrooms, ginger, garlic, soy sauce, MSG, and sesame oil and mix with clean hands until uniform in texture.

Set a small bowl of water on your work surface. Place the dumpling wrappers on a cutting board and use a small spoon to add about 2 teaspoons of the filling to the center of each wrapper.

This is the simplest way to fold: Dip a finger into the water and moisten the edges of the bottom half of the wrapper, then fold the top over the bottom, enclosing the filling while pushing out any trapped air. Press on the edges to seal. You can moisten and pleat the sealed edges, if desired. Repeat with the remaining wrappers.

Proceed to steam, boil, pan-fry, or deep-fry the dumplings following the instructions on pages 144 through 146. Serve with dipping sauce on the side.

Vegan Wonton Noodle Soup

Serves 4

Kosher salt
6 cups Vegan Broth (page 37)
24 Vegetable and Tofu Dumplings (see
    opposite page)
16 ounces noodles, any type
3 cups roughly chopped bok choy

Optional toppings: Basic or Fragrant Chili
    Oil (pages 44 and 45), Duo Jiao (page 55),
    doubanjiang, Ginger Scallion Oil (page 53)

Bring a large pot of lightly salted water to a boil.
Keep the broth at a simmer in a separate pot. Add
the wontons to the boiling water and cook for
4 minutes if fresh, or 8 minutes if frozen. Using a
slotted spoon, remove the wontons from the water
and divide them among four bowls.

Add the noodles and bok choy to the boiling water
and cook according to the package directions
until the noodles are tender, then drain. Divide the
noodles and bok choy among the bowls and cover
each with broth. Add the toppings to taste, or not,
and serve.

Spicy Beef Dumplings
(with a Vegan Dupe)

Makes 12 dumplings

1 tablespoon cornstarch

4 ounces ground beef (preferably 85% lean) or plant-based ground meat substitute

1 cup finely chopped fresh chives (preferably Chinese chives)

2 fresh red chilies (such as Thai, cayenne, or Fresno), stemmed and minced

2 teaspoons grated fresh ginger

2 garlic cloves, grated

2 tablespoons Shaoxing wine

2 teaspoons light soy sauce

1 teaspoon dark soy sauce

1 teaspoon freshly ground white pepper

1 teaspoon onion powder

1 teaspoon Five-Spice Powder (page 59)

12 dumpling wrappers, circular or square

Dumpling Dipping Sauce (page 146), for serving

Beef dumplings are great, as they complement strong-flavored spices and heat very well, and there's the added bonus that ground beef is much more common in North American grocery stores than ground pork. You can also substitute plant-based equivalents like Beyond Meat or Impossible brand in equal measures. (These are great in the Vegan Wonton Noodle Soup, page 153.) I like these boiled in a spicy broth or pan-fried with chili oil.

In a large bowl, mix the cornstarch with 2 tablespoons cool tap water until smooth. Add the ground beef, chives, chilies, ginger, garlic, wine, light soy sauce, dark soy sauce, white pepper, onion powder, and five-spice and mix with clean hands until uniform in texture.

Set a small bowl of water on your work surface. Place the dumpling wrappers on a cutting board and use a small spoon to add about 2 teaspoons of the filling to the center of each wrapper.

This is the simplest way to fold: Dip a finger into the water and moisten the edges of the bottom half of the wrapper, then fold the top over the bottom, enclosing the filling while pushing out any trapped air. Press on the edges to seal. You can moisten and pleat the sealed edges, if desired. Repeat with the remaining wrappers.

Proceed to steam, boil, pan-fry, or deep-fry the dumplings following the instructions on pages 144 through 146. Serve with dipping sauce on the side.

Shrimp Paste Dumplings

Makes 24 dumplings

1 cup shrimp paste (see page 67)
24 dumpling wrappers, circular or square
Dumpling Dipping Sauce (page 146), for serving
Black or red vinegar, for serving

Shrimp paste is a delicious dumpling filling on its own (I spread it over bread on page 67 for a classic Hong Kong shrimp toast), or with other proteins blended in (see Note). The paste is soft initially but firms up nicely as it cooks.

Chill the shrimp paste in the refrigerator for at least an hour or up to 2 days before using, so it firms up a little and is easier to work with.

Set a small bowl of water on your work surface. Place the dumpling wrappers on a cutting board and use a small spoon to add about 2 teaspoons of the shrimp paste to the center of each wrapper.

This is the simplest way to fold: Dip a finger into the water and moisten the edges of the bottom half of the wrapper, then fold the top over the bottom, enclosing the filling while pushing out any trapped air. Press on the edges to seal. You can moisten and pleat the sealed edges, if desired. Repeat with the remaining wrappers.

Proceed to steam, boil, pan-fry, or deep-fry the dumplings (steam recommended) following the instructions on pages 144 through 146. Serve with dipping sauce or black or red vinegar.

Note: To the basic shrimp paste recipe, add 4 ounces minced scallops (any type), minced boneless whitefish fillets, ground pork, or ground chicken.

Rangoons

The crunchy-fried cream-cheesy dumpling known as crab rangoon originated in San Francisco's campy Trader Vic's restaurant in the 1950s, and it quickly developed a passionate following. Since then, it's become a staple on American Chinese restaurant menus, and the term "rangoon" has sort of come to encompass any deep-fried wonton or dumpling with a cream cheese filling. Because the original rangoon never really subscribed to any sort of Chinese flavors (if anything, it was an attempt at Polynesian food), I let my imagination run wild with these. I asked myself, "Would this be good creamy and fried?" And then put it in.

Crab Rangoons

Makes 30 rangoons

8 ounces imitation crab (aka crab stick, crab surimi, or krab), diced
1 (8-ounce) block cream cheese, at room temperature
2 scallions, thinly sliced
2 teaspoons garlic powder
2 teaspoons light soy sauce
2 teaspoons chicken powder or MSG
1 teaspoon Worcestershire sauce
30 square wonton wrappers
Neutral oil, for frying
Dumpling Dipping Sauce (page 146), for serving

Like California rolls, which almost always include imitation crab, crab rangoons make good use of this often-maligned product that is made from fish and flavorings, not crab—it's just shaped and dyed to look like the meat you pull from crab legs. Once it's been mixed with cream cheese and spices, stuffed into a wonton wrapper, and fried, the delicate flavor of fresh crab would be overpowered, while the springy texture of imitation crab holds up well.

In a large bowl, mix the crab, cream cheese, scallions, garlic powder, soy sauce, chicken powder, and Worcestershire with a wooden spoon until the ingredients are evenly blended and there are no lumps of cream cheese.

Set a small bowl of water on your work surface. Place the wonton wrappers on a cutting board and use a small spoon to add about 2 teaspoons of the filling to the center of each wrapper.

This is the simplest way to fold, rangoon-style: Dip a finger into the water and moisten the edges of the wrapper, then bring each corner to the center, pressing the seams together so it makes a square shape with the seams forming four lines that radiate from the center. Repeat with the remaining wrappers.

Deep-fry the rangoons in oil following the instructions on page 146. Serve with dipping sauce on the side.

159

Buffalo Chicken Rangoons

Makes 30 rangoons

12 ounces shredded cooked
    chicken breast (see page 73),
    about 2 cups
1 cup Frank's RedHot hot sauce
1 (8-ounce) block cream cheese,
    at room temperature
1 tablespoon garlic powder
2 teaspoons onion powder
2 teaspoons cayenne pepper
2 teaspoons ground chipotle
    chili (optional)
2 teaspoons MSG
2 teaspoons kosher salt
2 teaspoons freshly ground
    black pepper
30 square wonton wrappers
Neutral oil, for frying
Blue cheese dressing
    (homemade or store-bought),
    for dipping

I was asked to make a snack for the Super Bowl and came up with these rangoons. This might have been the recipe that started me down this whole chaotic rangoon spiral. Tangy Buffalo chicken (feel free to add even more cayenne, if you'd like) is perfect with a blue cheese dressing.

In a large bowl, mix the chicken, hot sauce, cream cheese, garlic powder, onion powder, cayenne, chipotle (if using), MSG, salt, and black pepper with a wooden spoon until the ingredients are evenly blended and there are no lumps of cream cheese.

Set a small bowl of water on your work surface. Place the wonton wrappers on a cutting board and use a small spoon to add about 2 teaspoons of the filling to the center of each wrapper.

This is the simplest way to fold, rangoon-style: Dip a finger into the water and moisten the edges of the wrapper, then bring each corner to the center, pressing the seams together so it makes a square shape with the seams forming four lines that radiate from the center. Repeat with the remaining wrappers.

Deep-fry the rangoons in oil following the instructions on page 146. Serve with blue cheese dressing.

Chicken Tikka Masala Rangoons

Makes 30 rangoons

2 tablespoons neutral oil, plus extra for frying
½ large white or yellow onion, minced
1 teaspoon grated fresh ginger
2 medium garlic cloves, grated
1 tablespoon ground Kashmiri chili or sweet paprika
2 teaspoons ground coriander
1 teaspoon ground cumin
2 teaspoons garam masala
1 teaspoon ground turmeric
½ teaspoon cayenne pepper or Szechuan chili flakes
1 (6-ounce) can tomato paste
1 tablespoon light brown sugar
2 teaspoons kosher salt
1 (8-ounce) block cream cheese, at room temperature
12 ounces shredded cooked chicken breast (see page 73), about 2 cups
30 square wonton wrappers
Plain yogurt (not Greek), for drizzling
Whole cilantro leaves, for garnish

In this recipe, the Indian spices combined with the cream cheese remind me of creamy chicken tikka masala once cooked.

In a medium skillet, heat the oil over medium heat. Add the onion, ginger, garlic, Kashimiri chili, coriander, cumin, garam masala, turmeric, and cayenne and cook, stirring often, until the onion is translucent, about 5 minutes. Stir in the tomato paste and cook for about 2 minutes to thicken it and get rid of its raw flavor. Turn off the heat and let cool to room temperature, then transfer the mixture to a food processor, add the brown sugar and salt, and process to a paste. Add the cream cheese and process until smooth. Transfer to a bowl and mix in the chicken.

Set a small bowl of water on your work surface. Place the wonton wrappers on a cutting board and use a small spoon to add about 2 teaspoons of the filling to the center of each wrapper.

This is the simplest way to fold, rangoon-style: Dip a finger into the water and moisten the edges of the wrapper, then bring each corner to the center, pressing the seams together so it makes a square shape with the seams forming four lines that radiate from the center. Repeat with the remaining wrappers.

Deep-fry the rangoons in oil following the instructions on page 146. Just before serving, drizzle with yogurt and garnish with cilantro.

BBQ Pork Rangoons

Makes about 30 rangoons

1 cup ketchup
¼ cup apple cider vinegar
2 tablespoons light brown sugar
1 tablespoon Szechuan or
    Korean chili flakes
2 teaspoons kosher salt
2 teaspoons freshly ground
    black pepper
1 (8-ounce) block cream cheese,
    at room temperature
1 tablespoon bourbon (optional)
12 ounces cooked pulled pork
    (about 2 cups)
30 square wonton wrappers
Neutral oil, for frying
Dumpling Dipping Sauce
    (page 146), for serving

A conversation that happened:

> *Me: "Hey, how easy is it to find precooked smoked pulled pork?"*
>
> *Not Me: "I'd say it's pretty easy."*
>
> *Me: "Okay, I'm doing this then."*

That's where this recipe came from.

Vegans: You already know pulled jackfruit would be a gorgeous replacement for the pulled pork.

In a large bowl, mix together the ketchup, vinegar, brown sugar, chili flakes, salt, pepper, cream cheese, and bourbon (if using) with a wooden spoon until everything is evenly blended and there are no lumps of cream cheese. Mix in the pork.

Set a small bowl of water on your work surface. Place the wonton wrappers on a cutting board and use a small spoon to add about 2 teaspoons of the filling to the center of each wrapper.

This is the simplest way to fold, rangoon-style: Dip a finger into the water and moisten the edges of the wrapper, then bring each corner to the center, pressing the seams together so it makes a square shape with the seams forming four lines that radiate from the center. Repeat with the remaining wrappers.

Deep-fry the rangoons in oil following the instructions on page 146. Serve with dipping sauce on the side.

Pork and Shrimp Dim Sims

Makes 24 dim sims

8 ounces ground pork
8 ounces peeled and deveined
    raw shrimp (any size), minced
1 cup minced napa cabbage
2 shallots, minced (about
    6 tablespoons)
1 tablespoon light soy sauce,
    plus extra for serving
1 teaspoon toasted sesame oil
2 teaspoons freshly ground
    white pepper
2 teaspoons freshly ground
    black pepper
1 teaspoon kosher salt
1 large egg
1 tablespoon cornstarch
24 square wonton wrappers
Neutral oil, for frying (optional)

Dim sims are a dumpling of Chinese Australian origin. Invented in Melbourne in the 1940s by William Chen Wing Young (father of Aussie icon Elizabeth Chong), they are a larger, more rectangular (though sometimes squat and rounded) adaptation of Cantonese siu mai, and are a beloved snack, steamed or fried, throughout Australia.

In a large bowl, use your hands to mix the pork, shrimp, cabbage, shallots, soy sauce, sesame oil, white pepper, black pepper, and salt. In a small bowl, beat the egg and cornstarch together and use your hands to mix it into the meat mixture until well combined. Form the mixture into a ball and chuck it back into the bowl a few times to help get the air out. The filling should be firm and retain whatever form you give it. See below for filling and steaming instructions.

To serve, place two dim sim in a bowl with some soy sauce. Or, for a bit of Aussie service, add a splash of soy sauce to a small plastic to-go bag, then add the dim sim and eat them out of the bag.

How to Fill and Shape Dim Sims

Place a wrapper in your nondominant hand. With a fork, scoop out 2 tablespoons (yes, you're going to fill this thing up) of the filling. Place it in the center of the wrapper and squeeze the wrapper around it, forming a kind of tube/pouch and squeezing somewhat firmly while pulling the fork out. It sounds complicated, but it's easier than it seems. Fill. Wrap. Squeeze. Pull. Use your hands to press them into tall rectangular blocks with equal sides. Optionally, pinch just under the opening of the dim sim to make it look almost like it's puckering up at you.

Steam (see page 144) for 10 minutes, or until the filling is fully cooked (sacrifice one to check). Or deep-fry at 350°F for 4 minutes.

Ginger-Scallion Lobster Dim Sims

Makes 12 dim sims

8 ounces raw lobster meat, minced

1 cup minced napa cabbage

2 tablespoons Ginger Scallion Oil (page 53), plus extra for serving

3 scallions, thinly sliced

2 teaspoons grated fresh ginger

2 teaspoons freshly ground black pepper

1 teaspoon freshly ground white pepper

½ teaspoon kosher salt

1 large egg

1 tablespoon cornstarch

12 square wonton wrappers

Neutral oil, for frying (optional)

Zhenjiang black vinegar, for serving (optional)

Duo Jiao (page 55) or sambal, for serving (optional)

If you love ginger scallion oil (and lobster), you'll love these dim sims. You can also substitute raw shrimp for the lobster for a less expensive, equally delicious bite. You can obtain the meat from whole frozen lobster tails; just buy 12 ounces to make up for the shell weight.

In a large bowl, mix the lobster, cabbage, ginger scallion oil, scallions, ginger, black pepper, white pepper, and salt with clean hands until well combined. In a small bowl, use a fork to beat the egg and cornstarch together and add this to the mixture, again mixing with your hands until all the ingredients are evenly distributed. Form the mixture into a ball and chuck it back into the bowl a few times (this helps get the air out of the mix; unlike dumpling filling, dim sim filling should be firm and retain whatever form you give it).

Follow the instructions How to Fill and Shape Dim Sims on page 163.

Serve these with Zhenjiang black vinegar, more ginger scallion oil, a fermented chili paste like duo jiao, or sambal.

Shrimp and Pork Lumpia with Avocado Salsa

Makes 12 lumpia

4 ounces peeled and deveined raw shrimp (any size), minced
8 ounces ground pork
1 teaspoon grated fresh ginger
1 tablespoon toasted sesame oil
1 tablespoon oyster sauce
1 tablespoon fish sauce
3 garlic cloves, grated
2 medium carrots, grated
1 small kohlrabi, peeled and grated, or 1 cup grated broccoli stems
12 egg roll wrappers
Neutral oil, for frying
Avocado Salsa (recipe follows), for serving

Growing up, I had three favorite childhood snacks: fried chicken wings, lumpia (Filipino spring rolls), and turon, a kind of sweet fried fruit lumpia. Here I took that childhood favorite (which were inspired by Filipino lumpia Shanghai, the name given to common pork-based lumpia) and added a touch of creamy freshness and heat with a Mexican-inspired avocado sauce.

In a large bowl, using a wooden spoon or clean hands, mix together the shrimp, pork, ginger, sesame oil, oyster sauce, fish sauce, and garlic until it becomes a uniform paste. Combine the carrots and kohlrabi in a separate bowl and set aside.

Set a small bowl of water on your work surface. Place a wrapper on your work surface so it looks like a diamond with the bottom corner pointing toward you. Spread about 2 tablespoons of the filling off-center (closer to you) laterally in a thin log, and nestle 2 tablespoons of the carrot-kohlrabi mixture on top. Fold the bottom point up toward the center and then fold the sides in so the wrapper resembles an envelope, encasing the filling tightly. Moisten the far edges with water and continue rolling to give it a tight log shape; the edge will seal as you roll. The finished lumpia will be thin, no more than an inch in diameter. Repeat with the remaining wrappers.

Fill a pot with neutral oil to a depth of 3 inches and heat over medium-high heat to 350°F. Add a few lumpia (don't overcrowd the pot) and fry for about 4 minutes, until golden brown and crisp. Use tongs to transfer the lumpia to a paper towel–lined baking sheet or plate and repeat with the remaining lumpia. Serve with avocado salsa.

(recipe continues)

Kung Food

Avocado Salsa

Makes about 1½ cups

2 ripe avocados, halved and seeded
1 jalapeño, halved and seeded
½ shallot
2 tablespoons fresh lime juice
2 teaspoons kosher salt
1 teaspoon fish sauce
2 teaspoons sugar

Scoop the flesh from the avocado into a blender
and add the jalapeño, shallot, lime juice, salt, fish
sauce, sugar, and 1 cup water. Blend until smooth
and use as a dip or drizzle over the lumpia.

167

*When I was
really little I thought
Stevie Wonder was
saying "Ay! Jusko! To
say I love you." Which
is funny if you speak
Tagalog.*

The efficiency of rice as a source of sustenance has allowed populations whose diets are based on it to grow much larger than those with wheat-based diets (an acre of wheat can produce about 4 million calories, while an acre of rice produces 11 million). Growing up, this humble grain that has shaped whole civilizations would sit quietly 45 degrees to the left of all my dinner plates, ready to add substance to anything I chose from the lazy Susan in front of me.

"Every grain of rice left in your bowl is a pimple on the face of your future wife." I remember that being said a lot when I was a kid, from the grown-ups who wanted to make sure I finished all my food before leaving the table. It didn't mean much to me as a four-year-old, nor does it mean all that much to me now as there are no pimples on my boyfriend's face.

Rice + Congee

Saying "we have rice at home" to a child is heartbreaking. Saying it to yourself as an adult is a mantra.

Basic Clay Pot Rice
(Bo Zai Fan)

Serves 2

1 tablespoon light soy sauce
1 teaspoon dark soy sauce
½ teaspoon fish sauce
½ teaspoon sugar
1 teaspoon freshly ground white
   pepper
½ strip lap yuk (Chinese cured
   pork belly, aka Chinese bacon;
   see Note)
2 Chinese sausages (see Note)
1 cup long-grain white rice,
   rinsed and drained
Thinly sliced scallions, for
   garnish

In its most basic form, bo zai fan is simply lightly seasoned rice cooked in a clay pot. I love this classic combination of Chinese sausage and cured pork belly, but it can be made with Shaoxing wine–marinated chicken, beef, root vegetables, or anything that takes well to what would fall under the umbrella of "Asian casserole-style cooking." Master this form and then let your imagination wander. This recipe can be easily multiplied to accommodate bigger pots (you can find clay pots that hold as much as 16 cups cooked rice), but most personal-size pots fit about 1 cup uncooked rice, while still leaving room for the other things.

In a small bowl, stir together the light soy sauce, dark soy sauce, fish sauce, sugar, and white pepper and set aside.

Slice the pork belly into ¼-inch-thick slices. Cut the sausage on an angle into ½-inch-thick segments, rotating the sausage 180 degrees each time you cut so the pieces are almost triangular in shape.

Place a clay pot over low heat and add the pork and sausage. Cook, stirring occasionally, until they release their juices and fat, about 10 minutes. Add the rice and cook, stirring to coat with the fat, until the grains are opaque and glossy, about 3 minutes. Add 1¼ cups water, increase the heat to high, and bring the water to a boil. Immediately reduce the heat to low, cover, and simmer for 20 minutes, or until the rice is tender; if it's still a little firm, just let it sit off the heat, covered, until ready to serve.

Just before serving, uncover the rice and drizzle with the soy sauce mixture, fluffing it as you incorporate the sauce. Garnish with scallions.

Note: Lap yuk, Chinese cured pork belly, is sold in long strips, usually with several pieces per package. If you don't have access to it or don't want to hunt around for such a small amount, leave it out; other bacons don't make a good substitute since lap yuk is unsmoked and has sweet as well as salty flavorings. Chinese sausages, aka lap cheong or xiang chang, are thin, firm links, usually about 6 inches long. There are regional variations in size, weight, and flavors, but for this recipe, any lap cheong can be used.

Bo Zai Fan

Clay pot rice is a hug in earthenware. The rice and the fixings all cook together in a clay pot, sharing their best qualities with one another. This is where Chinese cured meats like sausages, pork belly, and ham truly shine. The rice absorbs the intense flavor of the meats and anything else it was cooked with, and the luckiest person at the table can help themselves to the crispy bits of charred rice waiting at the bottom of the pot. For true clay pot cooking, use a Chinese clay pot or a Japanese donabe. You can find them at large Asian supermarkets or online. You can get a good one for under $50, and as with any good pot, it will last forever if you take care of it.

Rice + Congee

Kung Food

"Clay Pot" Rice Tahdig

Serves 4 to 6

3 cups white basmati rice
Kosher salt
2 black cardamom pods
3 star anise pods
1 cinnamon stick
Small pinch of saffron threads
    (about 10; optional)
½ cup plain yogurt (not Greek)
Freshly ground white pepper
3 tablespoons ghee
5 Chinese sausages, sliced
    ½ inch thick (see Note,
    page 171)
2 strips lap yuk (Chinese
    cured pork belly; see Note,
    page 171), sliced crosswise
    ½ inch thick

I first witnessed tahdig being made on TikTok, and I was stunned by it. It's a Persian preparation that involves cooking rice in a nonstick stockpot to create a whole dome of beautifully scorched rice along the bottom. Inverted onto a plate, the gold crust was just magnificent. To me, this was a thing of beauty, because the scorched rice at the bottom of clay pots is almost universally regarded as the best part. I wanted to incorporate this method into the flavors of clay pot rice. This is meant to be a rice dish, not a stand-alone meal, so serve this along with anything you'd normally eat with rice. I would attempt this with only a nonstick stockpot.

Put the rice in a large bowl and cover with cool water. Swish it around with your hand until the water is cloudy, then drain the rice in a fine-mesh sieve and return it to the bowl. Repeat until the water is almost clear after swishing (this should take a minimum of three changes of water).

Bring a pot of water to a boil, adding enough salt that it tastes about half as salty as pasta water (this would be in the "pretty salty but not unbearably salty" realm). Add the rice, cardamom, star anise, cinnamon, and saffron threads (if using) and allow the water to come back to a boil, taking care not to let the pot foam over. Reduce the heat, if necessary, but keep things moving rather aggressively to get even coverage of the rice. Check a couple of rice grains after 7 minutes. They should be translucent and soft on the outside but a firm, opaque white in the middle; this is parboiled rice. Once it reaches this stage, use chopsticks or a small strainer to remove the saffron threads (which should be floating on top) and set them aside. Drain the rice in a fine-mesh sieve and rinse it under cold water to stop the cooking.

In a large bowl, stir together the yogurt, the reserved saffron threads, 1 cup of the cooked rice, and a large pinch each of salt and white pepper.

(recipe continues)

In a nonstick stockpot, heat the ghee over medium heat until sizzling hot, then press the yogurt-rice mixture over the bottom of the pot to start forming a crispy shell. Mix the rest of the cooked rice with the sausage and pork belly and layer this over the yogurt-rice layer.

Cover the pot with a clean, thin kitchen towel before putting on the pot lid. (This is to prevent droplets of condensation that form on the underside of the lid from falling back onto the rice.) Reduce the heat to low and cook for 45 minutes.

Raise the heat to medium-low and cook for 5 minutes before removing the pot from the heat; this will crisp the rice, while the low heat should prevent it from burning. Open the lid a crack to allow excess steam to escape during this stage. You should smell a toasty aroma at most. If you smell burning, there are parts of the rice that are burning and it should be taken off the heat. A little scorching is fine (and not unusual), but don't let it smoke! Smoke will give the entire dish an acrid burnt flavor. At this point, you can hold the rice at room temperature until you're ready to serve it.

Cover the pot with an inverted plate (make sure the plate's circumference is larger than the pot's) and then carefully flip the pot and plate over together with the intention that the cooked rice will release from the pot and fall onto the plate. If the rice doesn't release, try forcibly shaking the pot up and down while still on a plate, or check the sides to see if they can be separated with a chopstick. Ultimately, hopefully, you'll end up with a dome of crispy golden rice on the plate. This dish is drama from start to finish, and you don't have drama if there's no payoff, and there's no payoff without the risk of failure.

Serve with whatever you enjoy with rice.

A Clay Pot Inspired by Jollof Rice

Serves 4 to 6

2 large red bell peppers, roughly chopped

2 plump, watery tomatoes, or 4 plum tomatoes, roughly chopped

1 to 3 Scotch bonnet or habanero peppers, stemmed, halved, and seeded (use gloves or be very careful not to touch your eyes after handling!)

2 tablespoons neutral oil

1 medium white or yellow onion, diced

1 tablespoon curry powder (Muchi or Jamaican curry powder works nicely)

½ (6-ounce) can tomato paste

1 (2-inch) piece fresh ginger, peeled and grated

3 garlic cloves, grated

1½ tablespoons chicken bouillon powder

1 teaspoon freshly ground white pepper

1 teaspoon freshly ground black pepper

2 sprigs thyme

3 cups long-grain white rice, rinsed and drained

5 cups Herbal Chicken Broth (page 36)

4 whole cloves

3 star anise pods

2 tablespoons fennel seeds

Jollof rice is one of my favorite rice preparations, period. It's a vibrant and delicious dish that I had the pleasure of first trying while cooking for my friend Tunde at From Lagos, his Nigerian BBQ pop-up in Detroit's Mexicantown. I gorged myself on the rice. It was bright and spicy with tomato and pepper, and such a departure from the rice I know. I ate it along with dishes like egusi stew, suya-dusted beef, and a black-bean-and-coconut dessert, the name of which I can't remember, but it reminded me of red bean pudding.

I wouldn't make a jollof again until my friend and fellow Detroiter Tega asked me to make it for her birthday the year we both blew up on TikTok. I felt she was mostly joking, but I made it for her nonetheless, and she had no notes, so I assume it tasted good. I'm not trying to reinvent the dish, by any means; it's just my way of paying tribute to something I see as beautiful and marrying it to my clay pot, since it's my preferred vessel for cooking rice. If you haven't had the opportunity to try good celebratory jollof, you haven't yet properly lived.

In a food processor or blender, combine the bell peppers, tomatoes, and Scotch bonnet and process to a fairly smooth purée. Set aside.

In a wok or saucepan, heat the oil over medium heat. Add the onion and sauté, stirring frequently, until translucent, about 3 to 4 minutes. Add the curry powder to activate the spices and, once it is fragrant, add the tomato paste. Stir-fry until the paste is well incorporated with the onion, about a minute, then stir in the ginger and garlic, followed by the blended pepper purée, the bouillon, white pepper, black pepper, and thyme sprigs. Raise the heat to high and stir-fry until most of the water is cooked out, about 8 to 10 minutes. Watch out for splatters as the mixture thickens; this will stain a shirt.

(recipe and ingredients continue)

2 teaspoons Szechuan
   peppercorns
1 cinnamon stick
2 teaspoons kosher salt

Add the rice to this paste, stir to combine, and transfer to a clay pot or Dutch oven, then stir in the broth, cloves, star anise, fennel, Szechuan peppercorns, cinnamon, and salt. Bring the liquid to a boil over high heat, then reduce the heat to maintain a gentle simmer. Place a sheet of aluminum foil over the pot, then cover with the lid. Cook over low heat, rotating the pot occasionally to prevent hot spots, for 45 minutes, or until the rice is tender. Fluff the rice with a fork before serving.

Bring this to a barbecue because it goes great with grilled things.

Rice + Congee

Fried Rice

The trick to great fried rice is controlling the water. What this means is not using freshly steamed rice simply because its high water content makes for mushy fried rice. The way to avoid this is to use somewhat chalky day-old rice. Its dry texture is ideal for creating fried rice that is well structured and not mushy.

You need to take care when cooling rice because toxic mold can grow on cooked rice left unrefrigerated for over two hours. Because rice is starchy and moist, it's an ideal place for mold to form, and while the mold isn't toxic itself, the spores from the mold can potentially get you *very* sick. It's happened to me before, and I promise you it's not fun. Luckily, keeping the mold growth down is pretty easy to do.

Steam your rice and cool it down to room temperature as quickly as possible before putting it in the fridge to finish drying off safely. The easiest way to do this is to spread the cooked rice over a baking sheet and then, either using a hand fan, or a small flat cookie sheet and a tight grip, fan the rice till it cools to room temperature. (During the winter in Detroit, I'll bring the pan outside until it stops steaming.) Transfer the rice to a covered container and put it in the fridge to finish cooling, which takes a couple hours. Cooked rice will keep in the refrigerator for up to 3 days.

One thing to try when making fried rice is steaming your rice using chicken broth or another aromatic liquid instead of water. This gives it a nice depth of flavor, and while it's not completely necessary, it adds a little something extra that makes a difference in such a simple dish.

Garlic Fried Rice

Serves 2 to 4

2 tablespoons neutral oil
4 garlic cloves, grated
4 cups day-old rice (see
    page 178)
Kosher salt and freshly ground
    white pepper
Pinch of MSG

This easy recipe is a good way to get the rhythm of frying rice down without putting too much effort into things like chopping veggies or preparing meat. The only flavor addition is garlic, so the simplicity allows you to totally focus on the timing of the fried rice. It's a perfect side dish, since it's tasty on its own but can easily partner with any dish you'd serve with plain rice.

In a wok, heat the oil over medium-high heat. Add the garlic and cook until some of the smaller pieces start turning golden brown, about 2 minutes. Add the rice and stir-fry, coating the grains evenly with the oil, and season with salt, white pepper, and the MSG. Serve immediately.

Note: *If you're cooking rice specifically for garlic fried rice, consider making it with Superior Stock (page 38) for extra-punchy flavor.*

Mushroom and Tempeh Fried Rice

Serves 2 to 4

3 tablespoons neutral oil

1 medium white or yellow onion, roughly chopped

6 ounces mixed mushrooms, thick stems removed, thickly sliced

2 cups chopped peeled lotus root

1 (6- to 8-ounce) block tempeh, cut into ½-inch cubes

2 tablespoons Shaoxing wine

2 teaspoons mushroom bouillon powder

¼ teaspoon MSG

2 garlic cloves, grated

4 cups day-old rice (see page 178)

2 teaspoons light soy sauce, plus more if needed

3 scallions, thinly sliced

Pinch of freshly ground white pepper

At my farmers' market there's a stall that specializes in mushrooms. They forage some, they grow some, and they import some, and come late spring and summer, they have these great chestnut mushrooms that are so tasty and hard to find in a regular store. The stalks eat like asparagus, and the mushroom itself is sweet and nutty. It's my favorite mushroom to cook with and is especially good in fried rice. Unfortunately, we can't all get our hands on these things, so a mixed mushroom medley paired with cubes of tempeh makes a fried rice I like to serve when I know a vegan or vegetarian is in the party.

In a wok, heat 2 tablespoons of the oil over medium-high heat. Add the onion and mushrooms and stir-fry until they start to char, about 3 minutes. Transfer to a plate.

Add the lotus root and tempeh to the wok. Stir-fry until they start to brown, about 3 minutes, then add the wine and stir to deglaze the wok. Return the onion-mushroom mixture to the wok and add the mushroom bouillon and MSG.

Add the remaining 1 tablespoon oil, the garlic, and the rice, and stir-fry until everything is mixed well. Stir in the soy sauce, scallions, and white pepper, then taste, adding more soy sauce if necessary. Continue to stir-fry until the rice has even color and is sizzling-hot throughout. Serve hot.

Chicken Fried Rice

Serves 2 to 4

12 ounces boneless, skinless chicken breast, cut into ½-inch pieces

1 teaspoon baking soda

2 tablespoons neutral oil

3 garlic cloves, grated

1 cup frozen tricolor diced vegetable medley (corn, carrots, and green beans)

4 cups day-old rice (see page 178)

1 tablespoon light soy sauce, plus more if needed

1 teaspoon freshly ground white pepper

1 teaspoon kosher salt

¼ teaspoon MSG

Why spend a few minutes ordering takeout when you can spend way more time and effort making it yourself at home? Because sometimes it's just nice to do things, Jeff. But seriously, this is so easy, reasonably healthy, and a good use of frozen vegetables. Frozen veggies are packed at the height of their freshness and peak nutritional levels, and while I'd like to say that's the reason I'm using frozen veggies in this recipe, it's really because I don't want to make you chop carrots, de-kernel corn, and peel peas for fried rice. The baking soda treatment on the chicken is a technique called velveting—a simple method to make the meat more tender.

In a large bowl, toss the chicken with the baking soda and let sit for 30 minutes. Rinse the chicken well and pat dry.

Heat a wok over high heat, then add 1 tablespoon of the oil. Add the garlic and cook, stirring, about 15 seconds, just until fragrant, then add the chicken. Stir-fry until it's almost cooked through, about 4 minutes, then transfer to a plate.

Add the remaining 1 tablespoon oil and the vegetables to the wok. Cook for about a minute to thaw them out, then add the rice and return the chicken to the wok. Stir-fry until everything is hot, the chicken is cooked through, and some rice grains start to turn golden and crisp. Stir in the soy sauce, white pepper, salt, and MSG, then taste, adding more soy sauce if necessary. Serve hot.

183

Parmesan-Curry
Egg Fried Rice

Serves 2 to 4

2½ tablespoons ghee

3 large eggs, lightly beaten

1 tablespoon Japanese curry powder (S&B is a good brand to use)

3 garlic cloves, grated

1 tablespoon minced fresh ginger

5 scallions, white and green parts separated and thinly sliced

4 cups day-old rice (see page 178)

1 teaspoon kosher salt

¼ teaspoon MSG

2 tablespoons grated Parmesan cheese

A mild curry paired with Parmesan cheese is a flavor combination I first experienced in Japan, and it works so well as the basis of this fried rice. I added the egg in there for a little bit of heft. I fry it in ghee because it's so at home with curry and adds a richness to the rice and egg.

In a wok, melt 1½ tablespoons of the ghee over medium-high heat. Add about three-quarters of the beaten egg and scramble. As the egg solidifies, roughly chop it into little pieces with your wok spatula. Slip the cooked egg out and into a separate bowl.

Add the remaining 1 tablespoon ghee to the wok and stir in the curry powder to activate it. When it releases its aroma, after about a minute, add the garlic, ginger, and scallion whites, pushing and pulling it across the wok bottom a couple of times before adding the rice. Cook, stirring continuously, until the rice is fully warmed through, about 2 minutes, then return the cooked egg to the wok, add the salt and MSG, and stir-fry until fully incorporated.

Drizzle in the remaining raw egg and add the scallion greens, then quickly mix to incorporate. Transfer to a serving bowl and top with the Parmesan. Serve immediately.

Rice + Congee

Kung Food

Golden Egg Yolk Fried Rice

Serves 2 to 4

3 salted egg yolks (see
    headnote)
2 tablespoons ghee
6 garlic cloves, grated
2 teaspoons cumin seeds
4 cups day-old rice (see
    page 178)
Pinch of kosher salt
¼ teaspoon MSG
1 teaspoon freshly ground
    white pepper

Rich and flavorful, this rice works well alongside vegetables and mushrooms, and it stands on its own as a decadent little treat. Vacuum-sealed pre-cured salted egg yolks are available in Chinese groceries and are much more convenient than making your own; they also help this dish come together quickly.

Place a bamboo steamer basket over a pot of boiling water. Put the salted egg yolks in a small ramekin, place it in the steamer, cover, and steam for 15 minutes, or until the yolks are very firm and crumbly. Transfer to a small bowl and mash to a paste with a fork.

In a wok, melt the ghee over medium-high heat. When the ghee is hot, add the garlic and cumin and stir-fry until the garlic begins to toast, about 1 minute. Add the rice, salt, and MSG and stir-fry until very hot before adding the cured egg yolks and white pepper. Mix to fully incorporate and serve.

Nasi Goreng

Serves 2 to 4

2 tablespoons neutral oil

3 garlic cloves, grated

1 or 2 bird's-eye chilies or other hot red chilies, thinly sliced

2 boneless, skinless chicken breasts (about 12 ounces total), cut into ¼-inch-thick strips

4 tablespoons kecap manis

Kosher salt

1 medium white or yellow onion, diced

2 teaspoons shrimp paste (see headnote; preferably Thai shrimp paste; I use the Twin Chickens brand)

4 cups day-old rice (see page 178)

2 teaspoons kosher salt

½ teaspoon MSG

Optional toppings: 4 fried eggs, thinly sliced scallions, diced tomatoes, diced cucumbers, fried garlic, fried shallots, lime wedges

This famous—and gorgeous—Indonesian fried rice makes use of kecap manis (sweet soy sauce) and shrimp paste. It's often served with a sunny-side-up egg, which is a good excuse to make it for breakfast. Shrimp paste (sometimes labeled "shrimp sauce" and not to be confused with the stuff I spread on toast on page 67) is packed with pungent umami. It's used in many Southeast Asian recipes and is easily found in Southeast Asian groceries, as well as larger Chinese groceries and online.

Heat a wok over high heat, then pour in 1 tablespoon of the oil and heat until shimmering. Add the garlic and chilies and quickly stir-fry. Add the chicken and toss to coat, then add 1 tablespoon of the kecap manis plus a pinch or two of salt. Stir-fry for 3 to 4 minutes, until the chicken is almost completely cooked through. Transfer the chicken to a plate and return the wok to the heat.

Add the remaining 1 tablespoon oil and the onion and stir, scraping the bottom and sides of the wok to pull up any sticky bits from cooking the chicken. Add the shrimp paste and the remaining 3 tablespoons kecap manis. Stir well and add the rice, tossing to break up any lumps. Stir-fry until the rice is warmed through, about 2 to 3 minutes. Taste the rice and season with salt and MSG, then return the chicken to the wok and cook for 1 minute more, or until the chicken is fully cooked through. Place the fried rice on a serving platter, garnish with the optional toppings of your choice, and serve.

Rice + Congee

Three Brunch Bowls

When I was operating my kitchen studio as a secret Saturday brunch spot in Detroit, I would often serve these brunch-y rice bowls made from things I'd found at the farmers' market earlier that morning. These were the three most popular versions. While they are nice over plain steamed rice, I would switch between white rice and Forbidden Rice based on what I felt like that day.

To those who have been to my brunches, stop asking me if I'll ever do them again. They were very illegal.

Kimchi Chorizo
Brunch Bowl

Serves 2

4 ounces fresh Mexican chorizo (casings removed, if using links)
1½ cups kimchi, drained and chopped
2 tablespoons Basic Chili Oil (page 44)
¼ teaspoon Basic Szechuan Peppercorn Oil (page 46)
3 cups steamed rice
2 eggs, sous vide (see page 62), poached, or sunny-side up
1 scallion, thinly sliced

In a nonstick skillet, cook the chorizo over medium heat, using a wooden spoon to break it up as you cook, until browned and cooked through. Turn off the heat, and after it's cooled down a touch stir in the kimchi. Finish with the chili oil and Szechuan peppercorn oil and serve over rice, topped with the eggs and scallions.

Salmon Tartare
Brunch Bowl

Serves 2

12 ounces boneless, skinless salmon fillet (see Note)
3 cups steamed rice
1 scallion, thinly sliced
2 teaspoons toasted, hulled sesame seeds
2 eggs, sous vide (see page 62), poached, or sunny-side up
2 tablespoons ikura (salmon roe), optional but highly recommended
Japanese soy sauce or ponzu, to taste

Mince the salmon as finely as possible. Serve over rice, topped with the scallion, sesame seeds, eggs, and ikura, if using, with soy sauce or ponzu to taste.

Note: *If possible, find a Japanese market and buy salmon intended for sushi. Or just tell your fish guy what you intend to do with it so he knows you need a high-quality cut.*

Oyster Mushroom
Brunch Bowl

Serves 2

8 ounces oyster mushrooms (see Note)
2 quarts Master Stock (page 42)
4 thumb-size pieces fresh ginger, peeled and thinly sliced
3 whole cloves
2 star anise pods
3 cups steamed rice (this is quite nice over purple or Forbidden Rice)
2 eggs, sous vide (see page 62), poached, or sunny-side up
Kosher salt and freshly ground black pepper

Clean and cut the mushrooms, removing the woody base that connects them so the tender little "petals" are separated. Bring the master stock to a boil in a large saucepan or stockpot over high heat and add the mushrooms, ginger, cloves, and star anise. Return to a boil, then reduce the heat to low, cover, and simmer for 45 minutes. Strain out the mushrooms and spices, discarding the spices and reserving the stock.

Serve the mushrooms over the hot rice, topped with the egg and seasoned with salt and pepper to taste.

Note: *If you're planning a big brunch and want to make the mushrooms ahead, you can refrigerate them for up to 5 days and quickly stir-fry to reheat before using.*

Clockwise from top left: Salmon Tartare Brunch Bowl, Kimchi Chorizo Brunch Bowl, Oyster Mushroom Brunch Bowl

Congee

There's nothing I like to eat in the winter more than congee, a savory rice porridge that shares a spirit with oatmeal, grits, and polenta. It's meant to be somewhat bland on its own; the idea is to keep the base rice porridge mellow and add flavor though toppings (see my favorite toppings on page 195; any that may be unfamiliar are available in Asian groceries or online). As a child, I loaded mine up with a dusting of dehydrated pork floss, which is kind of like if bacon were cotton candy. Congee batches easily and stores fantastically in the fridge for a quick, reheatable meal.

If you want the congee to have a more pronounced flavor to begin with, add a little chicken or mushroom bouillon powder, or cook the congee using a stock of some kind like chicken, beef, pork, or duck.

Long-grain rice is my rice of choice for congee because of its versatility. You have the option with long grain to either get it down to a very soft and almost puddinglike consistency, or a lighter and more liquid congee with more individual grains still intact. Adding a little glutinous rice flour (about ½ teaspoon per 1 cup raw rice) will get you a creamy consistency while still maintaining the texture of some of the individual rice grains.

Washing the rice is important, because though all rice is starch, you want control over how that starch is released. Unwashed rice has a dusty coating of starch that dissolves immediately into the broth and can make it gummy. Also important is the fact that not all rice has been washed in processing, so rinsing before cooking keeps dust, bug segments, and mite eggs out of your congee. It probably won't hurt you if you don't wash the rice, but I feel it's worth the trouble.

One trick that my friend Joanne (also known as the Korean Vegan) learned from her mother and passed on to me was the use of oats as congee. The amount of fiber in oats made her stay fuller for longer, and it helped fuel her long-distance running. Now, you might be thinking, *That's literally just oatmeal*, and you'd be right, but congee can also be a mindset. For me, oatmeal was a sweet breakfast dish, and I associated that oaty flavor with sweetness. So to counteract that, I always add a little bit of chicken or mushroom bouillon powder to give oat congee a little nudge in the direction of the congee flavor I'm used to. The substitution for oats to rice is 1:1. As a bonus, you don't need to rinse oats before cooking, which to me was the most convincing thing about the substitution.

Some Favorite Congee Toppings

Sliced scallions
Cilantro leaves
Gan lan cai (Chinese preserved olive vegetable)
Pickled bamboo shoots
Ya cai (preserved mustard greens)
Lan chi (preserved chili radish)
Kimchi
Poached egg or hard-boiled egg
Fragrant Chili Oil (page 45)
Toasted sesame oil
Chili crisp
Sautéed mushrooms
Salted duck egg or century eggs
Youtiao (Chinese fried dough)

195

Youtiao in Cantonese is yau ja gwai, which means "fried ghost" and is what my boyfriend calls them really loud and in public. It's great.

Left to right: Beef Congee (page 199) with pickled jalapeño, Mushroom Congee (page 201) with chili oil, Fish Congee (page 198) with fried shallots, cilantro, and sliced scallions

Fish Congee

Serves 4

1 cup long-grain jasmine rice, washed (see page 194)

12 ounces boneless white-fleshed fish, such as cod, bass, snapper, or tilapia fillets, cut into 2-inch chunks

1 thumb-size piece fresh ginger, peeled and thinly sliced

2 teaspoons dashi powder, mushroom bouillon powder, or chicken bouillon powder (optional)

Kosher salt (optional)

3 scallions, thinly sliced, or ¼ cup packed fresh cilantro leaves

Congee fixings (see page 195)

Cooking white-fleshed fish fillets in congee breaks it down into little pieces and makes the congee itself even milkier. Adding dashi powder (a soup base derived from seaweed and fish) to the water leans into the oceanic angle. Scallions are great here, but I think the herbiness of cilantro (if you like cilantro) complements the fish nicely. Leave the ginger slices in the congee; they're easy to eat around.

In a large nonstick stockpot, bring 10 cups water to a boil over high heat. Add the rice, return the water to a boil, then reduce the heat to medium and cook, stirring often, until the congee has the consistency of loose porridge. You want the bubbles to constantly agitate the rice grains as the grains absorb the water; this releases the starch into the water and thickens it in the process. Adjust the heat if necessary to maintain this stage. Depending on the power of your burner and the size and shape of your pot, it may take anywhere from 30 to 45 minutes for the rice to break down and thicken the water properly.

When the congee has thickened to the right consistency, add the fish, the slices of ginger, and the dashi powder (if using). Cook, stirring occasionally, just until the fish is cooked through; this should take only about 5 minutes. The fish should flake and disperse into the congee as it cooks, but feel free to nudge it along so there will be a little fish in each bite. Taste and add salt if needed. Divide among bowls and finish with the scallions and any of your other favorite toppings.

Beef Congee

Serves 4

2 teaspoons beef bouillon or mushroom bouillon powder (optional)

2 (10-ounce/300 ml) pouches seolleongtang (Korean beef bone soup base; optional, but very worth finding)

1 cup long-grain jasmine rice, washed (see page 194)

8 ounces thinly sliced tender beef (such as tenderloin or rib eye) or *very* thinly shaved chuck or brisket (as thin as you would use for hot pot)

2 teaspoons light soy sauce

2 teaspoons grated fresh ginger, plus 1 thumb-size piece fresh ginger, peeled and thinly sliced

1 teaspoon freshly ground white pepper

1 teaspoon neutral oil

½ teaspoon potato starch

3 scallions, thinly sliced

Kosher salt (optional)

Congee fixings (see page 195), for serving

Beef congee is usually my default order when I'm trying a new congee place. It's more flavorful than chicken or pork congee, and the meaty slices are so satisfying. I also love the flavors of seolleongtang, a Korean beef bone soup base, which you can purchase in pouches at some Asian grocery stores. To me, it's a no-brainer, since seolleongtang is so milky and flavorful and gorgeously beefy. Be mindful that some seolleongtang packets are already seasoned and salted, so taste before adding additional salt. If using the seolleongtang, reduce the amount of water by however much broth is in the packet (and leave the beef or mushroom bouillon out of the recipe, too).

In a large nonstick stockpot, combine 10 cups water, the bouillon (if using), and the seolleongtang (if using) and bring to a boil over high heat. Add the rice, return the water to a boil, then reduce the heat to medium and cook, stirring often, until the congee has the consistency of loose porridge. You want the bubbles to constantly agitate the rice grains as the grains absorb the water; this releases the starch into the water and thickens it in the process. Adjust the heat if necessary to maintain this stage. Depending on the power of your burner and the size and shape of your pot, it may take anywhere from 30 to 45 minutes for the rice to break down and thicken the water properly.

Meanwhile, in a bowl, toss the beef with the soy sauce, grated ginger, white pepper, oil, and potato starch and let sit until the congee is almost done.

When the congee has thickened to the right consistency, add the beef mixture, sliced ginger, and scallions and stir well. Taste and add salt, if necessary. Serve topped with the fixings of your choice.

199

Your Friend, the Nonstick Stockpot

Because congee water gets very thick and starchy, there's a chance the congee will stick and burn onto the bottom of the pot as it cooks. As with rice, a burnt bottom layer will add an unpleasant, acrid smokiness to the whole batch. A nonstick stockpot prevents this from happening and also means you don't have to stir as often. Starchy soups, sauces, and curries also run the risk of burning this way, so a nonstick stockpot is quite a useful thing to have.

An alternative is to buy a higher-end rice cooker with a congee setting, which eliminates the need to babysit the pot. Instead, it's as easy as adding washed rice (or oats) and the appropriate amount of water, closing the lid, and pressing the button. You can do all this the night before and set it on a timer, then wake up to fresh congee. Unless I'm making a large batch or working with large ingredients like a whole turkey (see page 238), this is the way I make congee at home.

200

The rice cooker and the automatic pressure cooker teach us that some of the best cooking is the cooking you don't have to be there for.

Mushroom Congee

Serves 4

8 ounces morels or other fresh mushrooms, such as chestnut, shiitake, hen of the woods, black trumpet, or a mix

1 tablespoon mushroom bouillon powder

1 cup long-grain jasmine rice, washed (see page 194)

1 teaspoon kosher salt

Sesame oil (optional)

Congee fixings (see page 195), for serving

I once made morel congee for a dinner at the Studio (that's what we called my secret kitchen space in Detroit)—it was gorgeously nutty and as decadent as you'd expect. Morels are seasonal, special, and not always available, so sometimes I'll swap in a mix of fresh shiitakes, dried porcini, and even chestnut mushrooms, if I can find them. The congee itself might be a little on the brown side, but it's beautifully flavored.

With a dry dish towel, brush any dirt from the mushrooms. Remove only the toughest stems and slice the mushrooms into bite-size pieces, if necessary. Set aside.

In a large nonstick stockpot, combine 8 cups water and the mushroom bouillon and bring to a boil over high heat. Add the rice and salt, return the water to a boil, then reduce the heat to medium and cook, stirring often, until the congee has the consistency of loose porridge. You want the bubbles to constantly agitate the rice grains as the grains absorb the water; this releases the starch into the water and thickens it in the process. Adjust the heat if necessary to maintain this stage. Depending on the power of your burner and the size and shape of your pot, it may take anywhere from 30 to 45 minutes for the rice to break down and thicken the water properly.

When the congee has thickened to the right consistency, add the mushrooms and cook for 5 minutes, or until tender. Divide among bowls and season with sesame oil, if desired. Serve with the toppings of your choice.

> *Don't use a restaurant-size wok as a toboggan. I won't say I speak from experience because I'm pretty sure legally I can't.*

Stir-Fries

The key to stir-frying is following the correct sequence based on how fast things cook and when they need to be cooked. The process moves very quickly, so you'll find most of your time is spent getting ready to cook as opposed to actually cooking, which is great, because you can get the prep done beforehand and cook it later. Some of these recipes might seem long and daunting, but with advance prep, most of them come together quickly at the last minute.

Kung Food

A Wok-Fried Egg

Serves 1

2 tablespoons neutral oil
1 large egg
Bowl of steamed rice (or
    whatever you're eating your
    egg with)
Dark soy sauce, for serving

*When you're learning how to cook on something new, whether it's
an unfamiliar pan or a newer heat source like an induction burner,
I always say to see how you can cook an egg on it. They're relatively
affordable, and they do a great job of showing you how quickly the
heat works its way through the food. Also, most things are better
with a fried egg on it.*

Preseason your wok (see page 29), then heat the oil in the hot wok
over medium-high heat. Crack an egg into the wok and allow the
white to set and then crisp around the edges and bubble. Reduce the
heat to medium-low, and if you want to spoon some hot oil over the
top of the white before flipping the egg, you may do so, but a well-
seasoned wok will be nonstick enough for you to flip and quickly cook
the top of the white before sliding it onto a bowl of rice or whatever
else you're eating it with. Top with a few drops of dark soy sauce
and enjoy.

Stir-Fries

A Wok-Fried Omelet

Serves 1

3 large eggs
Pinch of kosher salt
¼ teaspoon freshly ground
    white pepper
2 tablespoons neutral oil
½ cup thinly sliced fresh garlic
    chives or scallions
Dark soy sauce, Kewpie mayo,
    and/or chili oil, for serving

Once you get the individual egg down, work on cooking a bunch of eggs. I like my omelets plenty runny and served over rice. Nothing fancy here, just folded in half, diner-style.

In a medium bowl, beat the eggs with the salt and white pepper.

Preseason your wok (page 29), then heat the oil in the hot wok over medium-high heat. Add the garlic chives and cook, stirring, for a few seconds, until they turn even brighter green. At this stage, you can transfer the chives to a bowl and use them to fill your omelet later or pour the eggs into the wok over the chives so they'll be mixed throughout the omelet. Either way, add the eggs and let them bubble and set on the bottom of the wok before flipping or filling the omelet and folding it in half. Transfer to a plate and serve immediately, garnished with dark soy, mayo, and/or chili oil to taste.

Stir-Fries

Chinese
Stir-Fried Potatoes

Serves 4

1 pound large red potatoes, peeled
¼ cup neutral oil
1 tablespoon minced garlic
2 teaspoons grated ginger
4 dried Szechuan chilies, roughly chopped
2 tablespoons Szechuan peppercorns
2 teaspoons distilled white vinegar or Zhenjiang black vinegar
2 teaspoons light soy sauce (optional)
Kosher salt to taste
Toasted sesame oil, for finishing
1 fresh red chili like a cayenne pepper, sliced

This is a fantastic dish that really doesn't get enough recognition in Western Chinese restaurants. It's just potato matchsticks wok-fried with Szechuan pepper, chilies, vinegar, and soy sauce or salt—but they're so damn good that they'll make you look at potato side dishes in a new light. I love them hot or cold and eaten with rice. While it might seem strange to eat two starches together, potatoes pair with rice really well. The mindset you need to have is that you're cooking these potatoes as you are a vegetable, not a starch. You want them to be fresh and crisp in the way that you'd treat a stir-fried slivered carrot or celery. This means with the potatoes being so thin, the cooking process is very quick. Using a mandoline here to julienne the potatoes is highly recommended.

Julienne the potatoes with a mandoline (as if you're making shoestring fries); otherwise, slice the peeled potatoes into ⅛-inch-thick planks by hand, then stack them and slice them lengthwise into ⅛-inch-thick strips. Soak the julienned potatoes in cold water for 20 minutes to remove some of the excess starch, then drain right before stir-frying.

Preseason your wok (page 29), then add the oil, garlic, ginger, chilies, peppercorns, and potatoes, in that order, stirring in between each a couple times to make sure everything gets even distribution of heat. Stir-fry the potatoes, coating them well with the oil, for 30 to 60 seconds; do not let them brown—you want them to be crisp like a nicely sautéed vegetable, not soft. Add the vinegar, soy sauce (if using), and salt, stir to coat, top with a hint of sesame oil and sliced red chilies, and serve immediately.

I've also had this dish cold, which was interesting. I read that cold potatoes develop gut-beneficial resistant starch. Jury's still out on whether day-old fries count.

208

Lomo Saltado

Serves 4

12 ounces store-bought frozen french fries, or more or less as desired

4 tablespoons neutral oil

1 pound sirloin steak, cut into thin, pinkie-size strips

½ Vidalia or other sweet onion, sliced crosswise

3 firm plum tomatoes, halved, seeded, and sliced into strips

1 tablespoon ají amarillo paste

¼ cup distilled white vinegar

1 tablespoon light soy sauce

2 teaspoons dark soy sauce

Kosher salt and freshly ground black pepper

Steamed rice, for serving

This Peruvian steak stir-fry is from Chifa cuisine, a fusion of Peruvian and Chinese cooking methods. I had the pleasure of having this dish in Lima, and it was so very good. Ají amarillo paste is made from a yellow Peruvian chili; it can be easily bought online and in some South American groceries. I highly recommend using store-bought frozen fries to save yourself the labor of deep-frying—then you can make the stir-fry while the fries are in the oven, turning this into a super-satisfying, quick-to-make meal. For the freshest fries, do all your prep, but don't actually start the stir-fry itself until 10 to 15 minutes before the fries are done.

Bake the fries according to the instructions on the bag. When they have about 10 minutes of cooking time left, preseason your wok (page 29), then heat 2 tablespoons of the oil in the hot wok over medium-high heat. Add the steak and cook until the surface of the meat has browned but the meat isn't yet cooked through, about 1 minute, then transfer to a plate.

Add the remaining 2 tablespoons oil and the onion to the wok. Cook for about 3 minutes, until they start to char, then reduce the heat to medium and add the tomatoes and ají amarillo paste. When the tomatoes soften, after about 2 minutes, add the vinegar and light and dark soy sauces, return the steak to the wok, and season with salt and pepper.

Top the mixture in the wok with the cooked fries (the quantity is purely up to you), then cover the wok and cook until the steak is done, about 2 minutes, depending on your doneness preference. Serve over rice.

Steak and (Chinese) Potatoes

Make the lomo saltado, but top it with Chinese Stir-Fried Potatoes (see opposite page) instead of the french fries. Garnish with fresh cilantro or sliced scallions.

Faygo Orange Chicken

Serves 4 to 6

Chicken and marinade

6 pieces dried tangerine peel, chopped

¼ cup Shaoxing wine

2 tablespoons light soy sauce

1 tablespoon ras el hanout

2 teaspoons ground cumin

¼ teaspoon MSG

2 teaspoons kosher salt

2 teaspoons freshly ground white pepper

2 pounds boneless skin-on chicken thighs, cut into roughly 1-inch cubes

Orange sauce

3 (12-ounce) cans orange Faygo or other orange soda

2 tablespoons Chinese red vinegar

⅔ cup sugar

2 teaspoons sweet paprika

2 teaspoons ground turmeric

3 star anise pods

2 black cardamom pods, cracked

4 pieces cup dried orange or tangerine peel, ground or minced

I was well into my thirties before trying the orange chicken from Panda Express, and randomly one day my curiosity got the better of me and I ordered some. It was fine. I'm not really in the business of being dramatic about food that's not for me, but something so iconic warranted some research. Orange chicken seems to have originated from a Hunanese dish called chen pi ji (orange peel chicken), in which pieces of chicken are flavored with orange peel and chilies. To accommodate local palates, I assume the spice was toned down and the sweetness was brought up. I wanted to bring it back to its origin story a little bit but respect the fact that—while this dish has relatives in China—orange chicken is an American icon, which is something I wanted to lean into. In a bit of a chaotic move, I decided to get the orange flavor from a Detroit local soda called Faygo (whose factory is not far down the street from the Studio). This recipe might look daunting, but it happens in stages; the chicken marinates for at least a few hours, and while that's happening, you can make the orange sauce and refrigerate it until you finish the dish later—or even the next day. You'll find quite a few dishes cooked in this style where proteins are fried and then sauced, and it's for a good reason: It produces delicious stuff. I double fry the chicken to maximize the crispiness (hat tip to the Koreans who figured this out for their fried chicken). Dried tangerine peel is easily available at Asian groceries or online.

Marinate the chicken: Place the tangerine peel in a spice grinder and pulverize it to a powder. You should end up with 2 teaspoons—put it in a large bowl with the wine, soy sauce, ras el hanout, cumin, MSG, salt, and white pepper and mix until well combined. Add the chicken and toss to evenly coat. Cover the bowl with plastic wrap and refrigerate for at least 2 hours and up to 12 hours.

Meanwhile, make the orange sauce: In a medium saucepan, combine the Faygo, vinegar, sugar, paprika, turmeric, star anise, cardamom, and orange peel. Bring to a boil over high heat, then reduce the heat to medium and cook until the sauce is thick and syrupy but

Frying

Neutral oil
3 cups all-purpose flour
3 cups potato starch
Kosher salt

Serving

2 tablespoons neutral oil
4 garlic cloves, grated
2 thumb-size pieces fresh
    ginger, peeled and minced or
    grated
2 to 4 dried Szechuan chilies,
    chopped
5 whole chilies for the drama
    (optional—but is it, really?)
2 tablespoons Szechuan
    peppercorns
1 tablespoon dark soy sauce
2 tablespoons Shaoxing wine
Steamed rice, for serving

still pourable, about 30 minutes, depending on the strength of your burner and the size and shape of your saucepan. Set the sauce aside. (The sauce can be cooled and stored in an airtight container in the refrigerator for up to a week.)

Fry the chicken: Fill a wok or Dutch oven with oil to a depth of 3 inches and heat the oil over medium-high heat to 350°F. Set a large wire rack nearby.

Combine the flour, potato starch, and 1 teaspoon salt in a large bowl. Working in batches, toss the chicken pieces in the flour mixture to coat well, then carefully add them to the hot oil (don't overcrowd the pot). Adjust the heat to maintain a temperature between 350° and 375°F and cook just until the chicken is very light golden brown, about 3 minutes (it won't be cooked through). Use a slotted spoon or spider to transfer the chicken to the rack to drain. Repeat with the remaining chicken pieces.

Again, working in batches, return the parcooked chicken to the hot oil and fry for 2 to 3 minutes, until it becomes a deeper golden brown—at this point, it'll be cooked through. Transfer the fully cooked chicken back to the rack to drain, and season with salt before it fully dries. Repeat with the remaining parcooked pieces.

To serve, once the chicken is cooked, heat a wok or very large sauté pan over medium heat. Add the oil, garlic, ginger, chopped chilies, whole chilies (if using), and Szechuan peppercorns and stir for only about 10 seconds before adding the dark soy sauce and the wine. Stir in the orange sauce and heat until it is thick and bubbling, about 5 minutes, then add the fried chicken and toss to evenly coat with the sauce. Serve immediately with rice.

Kung Food

Chipotle Mango Sweet-and-Sour Pork

Serves 2 to 4

Pork and marinade

1½ pounds pork tenderloin, cut into 1-inch cubes
½ teaspoon garlic powder
½ teaspoon onion powder
1 teaspoon toasted sesame oil
2 tablespoons light soy sauce

Sauce

1 cup distilled white vinegar, plus more (optional) as needed
½ cup ketchup
½ cup sugar, plus more (optional) as needed
1 tablespoon grated fresh ginger
2 star anise pods
2 chipotle peppers (from a can of chipotles in adobo), mashed to a purée with a fork

Frying

Neutral oil
½ cup all-purpose flour
½ cup tapioca starch or potato starch
½ teaspoon kosher salt
1 teaspoon freshly ground white pepper
2 large eggs

Not sure if you know this, but there is no actual pineapple in the sauce for sweet-and-sour pork. It's sweetened with sugar and made sour by vinegar, then the pineapple is added afterward. I'm not changing that part, but I am replacing the pineapple with mango and adding chipotle to the sauce because I enjoy smoky flavors (mezcal is my favorite spirit to make cocktails with and has been since I was twenty), and when you think of a sweet counterbalance to chipotle, you think of mango. But the main reason for me to make this dish at all was that my niece, Xing, asked me to make sweet-and-sour pork, and I said I would.

Marinate the pork: In a large bowl, combine the pork, garlic powder, onion powder, sesame oil, and light soy sauce with clean hands. Cover and refrigerate for at least 2 hours and up to 24 hours.

Make the sauce: In a small saucepan, combine the vinegar, ketchup, sugar, ginger, star anise, and chipotles and cook over medium heat, stirring often, until the sauce becomes thick and syrupy but is still pourable, about 30 minutes. Adjust the flavors with additional vinegar or sugar, if desired. (The sauce can be cooled and stored in the refrigerator, tightly covered, for up to a week.)

Fry the pork: Fill a wok or Dutch oven with oil to a depth of at least 3 inches and heat the oil over medium-high heat to 350°F. Have a wire rack or a paper towel–lined baking sheet nearby.

In a medium bowl, mix the flour, tapioca starch, salt, and white pepper. Lightly beat the eggs in another medium bowl and set it next to the flour mixture.

Working in batches, use chopsticks to toss a few of the pork pieces in the egg, letting any excess drip off, then coat in the flour mixture and add to the hot oil. Adjust the heat to maintain a temperature

(recipe and ingredients continue)

To finish

1 ripe mango, pitted, peeled, and
    cut into ½-inch chunks
1 tablespoon Tajín seasoning
1 tablespoon neutral oil
½ large red onion, chopped
1 red or yellow bell pepper
    (or ½ of each for color
    variation), chopped
Steamed rice, for serving

between 350° and 375°F and fry until very light golden brown, about 2 to 3 minutes (the pork won't be completely cooked through). Use chopsticks or tongs to transfer to the rack or paper towels to drain and repeat with the remaining pork.

When all the pork is cooked, return the first batch of parcooked pork to the oil and cook for 2 to 3 minutes, until it becomes deeper golden brown and is fully cooked through (cut into a piece to make sure). Transfer the fully cooked pork back to the rack or paper towels to drain and repeat with the remaining parcooked pork.

Finish the dish: In a small bowl, toss the mango with the Tajín and set aside. In a wok or very large sauté pan, heat the oil over medium-high heat. Add the onion and bell pepper and stir-fry until they start to char, about 3 to 5 minutes. Add half the sauce and let it bubble to a thick glaze consistency. Just before serving, add the fried pork and mango, adding additional sauce if necessary to lightly coat the pork. Serve with rice.

Mongolian Beef

Serves 4

1 tablespoon potato starch, plus
more for dredging

3 tablespoons light soy sauce

1 tablespoon dark soy sauce

5 tablespoons Shaoxing wine

8 ounces flank steak, cut against
the grain into thin, pinkie-size
strips

3 tablespoons chicken stock

1 tablespoon light brown sugar

2 tablespoons neutral oil

3 garlic cloves, grated

2 fresh red chilies (such as Thai,
cayenne, or Fresno), stemmed
and minced

Steamed rice, for serving

Toasted hulled sesame seeds,
for garnish

A favorite dish of American Chinese restaurants, Mongolian beef originated in Taiwan (along with "Mongolian barbecue" restaurants). In the US, it often has a sweet thick sauce; playing on that, I wanted to tone it down a touch and pair it with Lebanese and Arabic flavors like toum, one of my favorite condiments. It's a pungent garlic sauce that's great on a grilled meat pita or as the best pairing for fries. If you're lucky enough to live in a place where you can buy prepared hummus and toum (such as Detroit), then by all means support your local grocer and do it. Making it yourself is great, but you're not going to make it better than they make it.

In a large bowl, mix the potato starch, 1 tablespoon of the light soy sauce, 1½ teaspoons of the dark soy sauce, and 3 tablespoons of the wine. Add the beef and toss to coat. Set aside to marinate for 30 minutes.

In a small bowl, whisk together the remaining 2 tablespoons light soy sauce, 1½ teaspoons dark soy sauce, 2 tablespoons wine, the stock, and the brown sugar until the sugar dissolves. Set this sauce aside.

In a wok, heat the oil over high heat.

Place about ½ cup potato starch on a large plate. When the oil is hot, toss the steak in the potato starch to lightly coat, shake off any excess, and add it to the wok. Stir-fry until the steak is nicely charred and takes on a sheen, 3 to 5 minutes. Transfer the beef to a plate.

Add the garlic and chilies to the wok, stir briefly, then add the sauce mixture, scraping up any browned bits from the bottom of the wok. The sauce should thicken quickly; when it does, return the beef to the wok and stir to coat. Serve over rice, garnished with sesame seeds.

Mongolian Beef
Pitas with Toum

Serves 2 (makes about 1½ cups toum)

Toum

½ cup garlic cloves (freshly peeled)
2 tablespoons fresh lemon juice
1 teaspoon kosher salt
1½ cups neutral oil

Pitas

Mongolian Beef (page 219)
2 fluffy pitas
4 tablespoons hummus
Large romaine lettuce leaves, roughly torn
Thinly sliced sweet onion, for serving
Fresh parsley or cilantro leaves, for serving

Toum is an intense Middle Eastern garlic sauce, something like a very garlicky Lebanese aioli. The best way to combat the garlic breath that comes from eating toum is to make sure everyone else around you is also eating toum. If everyone has garlic breath, no one has garlic breath.

Make the toum: In a small food processor or high-speed blender, combine the garlic, lemon juice, and salt and purée to make a very smooth paste. With the machine running, very slowly add the oil through the feed tube, as if you're making mayonnaise, adding 1 tablespoon water after each ½ cup of oil. You should end up with a fluffy emulsified garlic sauce. If not using immediately, refrigerate the toum in an airtight container for up to 3 days.

Assemble the pitas: Prepare or reheat the Mongolian beef. Split the pitas open and spread the inside of each with 2 tablespoons of the hummus. Add some lettuce, onion, and beef. Drizzle 2 tablespoons of the toum over the top and garnish with parsley or cilantro.

Kung Food

Ginger Beef

Serves 4

Steak and marinade

2 tablespoons grated fresh ginger
2 tablespoons light soy sauce
1 teaspoon freshly ground white pepper
1 pound flank steak or boneless beef short ribs, cut against the grain into thin, pinkie-size strips

Sauce

¼ cup light soy sauce
1 tablespoon dark soy sauce
2 tablespoons rice vinegar
⅔ cup lightly packed light brown sugar

Batter

Neutral oil, for frying
2 cups all-purpose flour
1 cup potato starch
2 teaspoons Five-Spice Powder (page 59), or use store-bought
2 teaspoons freshly ground white pepper
1 teaspoon kosher salt
2 large eggs

To finish

1 tablespoon neutral oil
1 tablespoon grated fresh ginger
3 dried Szechuan chilies or other hot red chilies, chopped
3 garlic cloves, grated
3 scallions, thinly sliced, for garnish
Steamed rice, for serving

A Chinese Canadian classic, beefy flank steak is marinated with ginger and white pepper for an hour, coated in a light batter, and fried until crispy, then tossed with a sweet-and-salty glaze flavored with garlic and fresh ginger. It's almost like a brighter warming variation of Mongolian Beef (page 219), familiar but distinctly different.

Marinate the steak: In a medium bowl, mix together the ginger, light soy sauce, and white pepper. Add the steak, toss to coat, and refrigerate for 1 to 2 hours.

Meanwhile, make the sauce: In a medium bowl, whisk together the light soy sauce, dark soy sauce, vinegar, and brown sugar until the sugar dissolves. Set aside.

Batter and cook the steak: Fill a wok or Dutch oven with oil to a depth of at least 2 inches and heat over medium-high heat to 350°F. Have a wire rack or paper towel–lined baking sheet nearby.

In a large bowl, whisk together 1 cup of the flour, the potato starch, five-spice, white pepper, salt, eggs, and 1 cup cold water. Place the remaining 1 cup flour on a large plate.

Remove the beef from the marinade. Working in batches, dredge it in the plain flour (this will make it easier for the batter to stick to the beef). Dip the beef in the batter to coat, letting any excess fall back into the bowl, then add it to the hot oil (do not overcrowd the pot). Cook until golden brown, about 3 minutes, checking the temperature of the oil often to make sure it stays between 350° and 375°F. Use a slotted spoon or spider to transfer the fried beef to the rack or paper towels, then repeat with the remaining beef.

Finish the dish: In a clean wok or large sauté pan, heat the oil over medium-high heat. Add the ginger, dried chilies, and garlic and stir-fry until fragrant, about 30 seconds. Add the sauce and bring to a boil, then add the beef and toss to coat. Garnish with the scallions and serve over rice.

Szechuan Paneer
with Mexican Chiles

Serves 4

Chile sauce

1 ancho chile, stemmed
2 guajillo chiles, stemmed
4 dried chiles de árbol, stemmed
Boiling water
¼ cup neutral oil
2 tablespoons grated fresh
    ginger
¼ cup minced garlic (about
    12 cloves)
2 tablespoons tomato paste
2 tablespoons distilled white
    vinegar
2 tablespoons light soy sauce
1 tablespoon sugar
1 teaspoon freshly ground white
    pepper
¼ teaspoon kosher salt

Paneer

2 cups all-purpose flour
¼ cup potato starch
2 teaspoons Five-Spice Powder
    (page 59)
2 teaspoons freshly ground
    white pepper
1 teaspoon kosher salt
Neutral oil, for frying
1 (8-ounce) block paneer, cut into
    ½-inch cubes (about 1 cup)
¼ cup packed fresh cilantro
    leaves, for garnish

I've been expanding my use of chiles beyond the Chinese varieties lately. Mexican chiles are widely available here in the US, and I really enjoy mixing and matching them to see what they do to the flavor of a dish that typically includes chiles from other parts of the world. Remove the seeds from the chiles if you want something more mild or leave them in for funsies.

Make the chile sauce: Remove seeds from chiles if desired. Place the ancho, guajillo, and árbol chiles in a large heatproof bowl and cover with boiling water. Soak for 30 minutes, until they are supple and rehydrated. Transfer to a blender with a few splashes of their soaking water (just enough to keep the blades turning), purée to a paste, and set aside.

In a wok, heat the oil over medium-high heat. Add the ginger and garlic, and stir-fry until fragrant, about 15 seconds, then stir in the chile paste and ½ cup water. Reduce the heat to low and simmer, without stirring, until oil floats to the top of the chili mixture, about 15 minutes. Add the tomato paste, vinegar, soy sauce, sugar, white pepper, and salt and mix well. Transfer to a bowl and set aside. (The sauce can be cooled and stored in the refrigerator, tightly covered, for up to 1 week.)

Make the paneer: In a large bowl, whisk together 1 cup of the flour, the potato starch, five-spice, white pepper, salt, and 1¼ cups cold water. Place the remaining 1 cup flour on a large plate.

Pour half the sauce into a large sauté pan and keep warm over low heat. Have the remaining sauce ready to be added to the pan, if necessary.

(recipe continues)

225

226

Kung Food

Fill a wok or Dutch oven with oil to a depth of at least 2 inches and heat over medium heat to 350°F. Have a wire rack or a paper towel-lined baking sheet nearby.

Working in batches, toss the paneer in the plain flour to coat on all sides, then, using chopsticks or fingers, dip it into the batter to lightly coat, letting any excess drip off, and add it to the hot oil. Fry until deep golden brown, about 3 minutes. Use a slotted spoon or spider to transfer to the rack or paper towels to drain. Transfer the fried paneer to the pan with the sauce and toss to coat, adding more sauce if necessary to fully coat the paneer.

Transfer to a platter and garnish with the cilantro. Serve immediately.

Spice tolerance isn't anything anyone is born with. It takes practice. The more you practice, the more spice you can enjoy.

227

Mapo Paneer

Serves 2 to 4

1 tablespoon fermented black beans, rinsed

¼ cup Lapsang souchong tea leaves

4 cups boiling water

12 ounces (usually 2 blocks, depending on brand) paneer, cut into ½-inch cubes

2 tablespoons neutral oil

5 dried Szechuan chilies or other hot red chilies

1 tablespoon Szechuan peppercorns

4 ounces ground beef (preferably 85% lean) or ground lamb

2 tablespoons doubanjiang (Chinese broad bean chili paste)

2 tablespoons Duo Jiao (page 55)

2 cups Herbal Chicken Broth (page 36), Superior Stock (page 38), or Vegan Broth (page 37)

3 tablespoons cornstarch

Kosher salt

2 scallions, thinly sliced, for garnish

Chinese and Indian cuisines are two of my favorites, so it made sense to me to make mapo tofu with the mild but texturally lovely paneer instead (also, I like the way "mapo paneer" sounds). Soaking the paneer in a warm bath of Lapsang souchong tea softens it and adds a smoky depth to the cheese. This is equally good as a side dish or a light main dish served over rice. I hate when a restaurant tries to make mapo tofu into a vegan dish by simply omitting the ground meat and thinking that's all they need to do. It's never good, tasting acrid and hollow because the ground meat was used as a fatty counterbalance for all the other flavors. If you're going to take away from the dish to make it vegan, you need to add something more.

Put the fermented black beans in a small bowl, cover with warm tap water, and set aside for 30 minutes, then drain and chop.

While the beans soak, put the tea leaves in a separate medium heatproof bowl and cover with the boiling water. Let steep until the tea is dark and strong, about 10 minutes, then add the paneer and set aside to marinate until the rest of the dish is assembled.

In a wok, heat the oil over medium-high heat. Add the chilies and Szechuan peppercorns and stir-fry until fragrant and crispy, about 1 minute. Turn off the heat and use a large spoon to transfer the chilies and peppercorns to a cutting board. Finely chop to a sandy texture (or grind them with a mortar and pestle instead).

Increase the heat under the wok to medium-high and add the ground beef, stir-frying until almost cooked through, about 2 minutes. Add the doubanjiang, duo jiao, and chopped fermented black beans. Stir to mix and add 1 tablespoon of the chopped chili-peppercorn mixture, then add the broth and bring to a gentle boil.

228

You can actually get high on food if it's spicy enough . . . so there's that.

In a small bowl, stir together the cornstarch and 3 tablespoons water. When the sauce comes to a gentle boil, add the cornstarch slurry 1 tablespoon at a time to thicken the sauce until very thick but still pourable.

Using a slotted spoon to leave the tea behind, transfer the marinated paneer to the wok and turn off the heat. Stir gently to coat; taste and add salt and/or more of the chili-peppercorn mixture if needed, then serve, garnished with scallions.

Stir-Fries

Smoky Tomato-Egg Stir-Fry

Serves 2

6 large eggs
2 teaspoons Tomato Soy Sauce
(page 52) or light soy sauce
2 teaspoons sugar
1 teaspoon toasted sesame oil
3 tablespoons neutral oil
2 teaspoons ground cumin
4 plum tomatoes, quartered
lengthwise
1 teaspoon freshly ground white
pepper
2 teaspoons smoked paprika
2 tablespoons Shaoxing wine
Steamed rice, for serving
2 scallions, thinly sliced

Topping (choose one): a splash of
Tomato Soy Sauce (page 52),
a splash of dark soy sauce, or
a bloop of Duo Jiao (page 55)

Stir-fried tomatoes and eggs are a quintessential home-cooked Chinese dish loved by kids and adults alike. For variety we add a bit of smoked paprika and cumin, which give it a smoky, earthy flavor that's a little reminiscent of shakshuka.

In a medium bowl, using chopsticks, whisk the eggs with the tomato soy sauce, sugar, and sesame oil. Set aside.

In a wok, heat 1 tablespoon of the neutral oil over high heat, then stir in the cumin and cook until it releases its fragrance, about 30 seconds. Add the tomatoes, white pepper, and paprika and stir-fry until the tomatoes soften and char, about 2 to 3 minutes. Add the wine, stir to deglaze the pan, and transfer the mixture to a plate, taking a little extra care to scrape your wok clean.

Add the remaining 2 tablespoons oil to the wok and swirl to coat, followed by the eggs. As the eggs cook, they'll create a large, flat mass, with the part in contact with the wok cooking faster than the egg that floats on top. Gently scrape and push aside the cooked egg to allow the still-liquid egg to run beneath it. Wait half a second and then scrape and push again. Once most of the egg has been cooked, return the tomato mixture to the pan and gently mix everything together. Cook to briefly reduce any liquid before dividing the stir-fry among bowls of steamed rice. Garnish with the scallions and let guests choose the topping of their choice.

Stir-Fries

People assume that kung fu is the practice of martial arts, when really it refers to any discipline that requires patience, energy, and time to complete. *Kung* (功) roughly translates to "hard work or skill," and *fu* (夫) to "time spent." When you say someone has "good kungfu," you're recognizing the work and the effort they put in. The dishes in this chapter are more time-consuming, and possibly more challenging, than those in the rest of the book. They're best suited to special events, holiday spreads, or maybe if you just want to give yourself a bit of an indulgence or a challenge one weekend. These are the dishes that impress at the table, that show off the patience, energy, and time you took to cook.

The kung in kung fu is not the same as the Kung in my name. In Swedish kung means king.

Kung Fu Means "With Effort"

Curry Mac and Cheese

Serves 6 to 8

Kosher salt

16 ounces pasta (preferably cavatappi or conchiglie)

11 tablespoons unsalted butter

1½ teaspoons smoked paprika

2 teaspoons garlic powder

1½ teaspoons onion powder

1 teaspoon freshly ground black pepper

1 teaspoon freshly ground white pepper

3 to 4 tablespoons Japanese curry powder (S&B Curry is perfect for this)

⅔ cup all-purpose flour

7 cups half-and-half

4 ounces Wisconsin brick cheese, grated (about 1 cup)

4 ounces extra-sharp cheddar cheese, grated (about 1 cup)

4 ounces Gruyère cheese, grated (about 1 cup)

1 cup panko bread crumbs

In Japan, the combination of mild curry flavors and cheese is a common one, and very popular. You'll find the combo in cheese-stuffed curry bread and baked curry rice covered in melted cheese. I took the idea and applied it to a hearty pan of baked mac and cheese. You can use any kind of pasta you prefer, but I highly favor cavatappi for its elongated, twisting macaroni-like shape, which adds a touch of elegance. Or consider using conchiglie (shells), because they do a great job of tucking the sauce into themselves for an extra-creamy bite. Wisconsin brick cheese is the cheese of choice for Detroit's famous Buddy's Pizza, the original Detroit-style pizza establishment. They use it because it melts like mozzarella but has more flavor, which is also why I use it here.

Cook the pasta in lightly salted water according to the package instructions until it's just underdone, usually 6 to 7 minutes (the pasta will continue to cook in the oven). Drain the pasta and transfer to a bowl. Rinse with cold water to stop the cooking and clean off the excess starch, cover with a damp paper towel, and set aside.

Preheat the oven to 350°F. Grease a 12-inch cast-iron skillet or a 9 by 13-inch baking dish with 1 tablespoon of the butter.

In a small bowl, combine 2 tablespoons salt, the paprika, garlic powder, onion powder, black pepper, and white pepper and set aside.

In a large pot, melt the remaining 10 tablespoons butter over medium heat until it starts to bubble. Stir in the curry powder and cook until it's aromatic, about a minute. Add the flour and whisk it into the butter until it's a uniform paste. While whisking, slowly pour in the half-and-half. Bring to a simmer, whisking continuously and ensuring there aren't any lumps, and cook until the sauce is bubbling and thick, about 10 minutes. Stir in the salt mixture, then add ½ cup of the brick cheese, ½ cup of the cheddar, and ½ cup of the Gruyère and stir until they've fully melted into the sauce.

Curry Powders

I've found that when mixing curry with cheese the spices to avoid are cardamom, ginger, and celery root. These more acrid flavors clash with the richness of Western cheese so look for curry powder that either doesn't include them or has them only at the end of the list of ingredients (ingredients are listed in order of highest to lowest concentration). Japanese S&B Curry is a great mild curry to use in combination with cheese.

Add the cooked pasta to the sauce and use a silicone spatula to gently fold it in, taking care not to break the pasta. (Depending on the type of pasta you use, you might find yourself with an extra-saucy mac—not a bad thing.)

Pour the mac and cheese into the prepared skillet, evenly distributing it with the spatula. There may be some pooling cheese sauce, which is fine; it will bake into the pasta. Top with the remaining brick, cheddar, and Gruyère cheeses, then sprinkle the panko on top.

Bake for 25 to 35 minutes, until the mac and cheese is bubbling and the topping is golden. Remove from the oven and serve immediately.

James Hemings invented American mac and cheese. He was also the first French-trained chef from America. He was Sally Hemings's older brother.

Kung Fu Means "With Effort"

Thanksgiving Turkey Congee

Serves 6 to 8

Reserved skin and bones from
1 turkey or 2 chicken
carcasses

Kosher salt

2 cups long-grain white rice
(such as jasmine), washed
(see page 194)

1 (3-inch) piece fresh ginger,
peeled and thinly sliced

3 cups shredded cooked turkey
or chicken (about 1 pound)

3 teaspoons glutinous rice flour
(optional)

Optional toppings: thinly sliced
scallions, soft- or hard-boiled
eggs, pickled bamboo shoots,
kimchi, chili oil, preserved
chili radish, any sweet-
pickled vegetable, additional
shredded roast meat (duck,
rotisserie chicken, roast
goose), gan lan cai (Chinese
preserved olive vegetable)

*My first experience with the Traditional American Holiday Spread
(aka Thanksgiving) came in the form of cartoons; specifically,* Mickey's
Christmas Carol. *It was the first rendition of the Dickens story I'd
ever seen, and also the first time I can remember wanting to eat
something that was on TV: turkey. The glittering Technicolor images
of food surrounding Scrooge McDuck as he squabbled with the Ghost
of Christmas Present were how I imagined all Americans celebrated
Christmas dinner. It wasn't until we moved to Canada a few years later
that I learned that life and food aren't what the cartoons make them
out to be. Life is harsh, Santa isn't real, and turkey is dry.*

*I also learned that the best part of the holiday centerpiece is actually
what's left over—the carcass. It's the part that I would fight over: the
roasted bones, unpicked meat, and crusted-on herbs and oniony bits.
You can use the carcass to make all kinds of things, but I suggest you
hold it for congee. In the off-season, make this with a store-bought
rotisserie chicken.*

Put the carcass(es) and 6 quarts (24 cups) water in a large
(preferably nonstick) pot. Bring to a boil over high heat, then reduce
the heat to low and simmer, uncovered, for an hour (don't bother
skimming, as the clarity of the broth is not a priority). At this point,
the broth should have a recognizable, if mild, roast turkey flavor.
If not, simmer until it does.

Season the broth with salt to taste, starting with 1 teaspoon at a time;
you should end up with a flavorful, slurpable broth. Strain the broth
and return it to the pot (discard the solids). You want to end up with
18 cups of broth; if you have more, save the extra for another use; if
you have less, make up the difference with water or chicken stock.

Add the rice and ginger to the broth and bring to a boil over high heat. Add the shredded meat and reduce the heat so the broth is at a brisk simmer. If using glutinous rice flour for a creamier congee, put it in a small bowl and whisk with ½ cup cold water to form a slurry, then add this to the broth and stir to incorporate. Simmer for about 1 hour, stirring often to prevent the rice from sticking to the bottom of the pot and burning, until the congee is creamy, the water has been completely absorbed by the rice, and the rice has broken down.

To serve, ladle the congee into bowls and garnish as desired with the optional toppings.

In Hong Kong they celebrate American Thanksgiving as a niche novelty holiday. That's where I learned that olive vegetable is pretty good in stuffing.

Kung Fu Means "With Effort"

Anatomy of a Hot Pot Party

My hot pot parties are pretty spectacular to behold: five boiling pots of broth running down a 16 by 4-foot table piled with all sorts of delicious things to cook in them. All you really need for medium to large gatherings are a couple of pots of boiling broth (I like to do one spicy and one mild, or one to cook meat and one to cook vegetables so it's easy to accommodate vegetarians and vegans) and a bunch of meats, tofu, and vegetables for everyone to cook as they like. I usually purchase everything at a Chinese grocery store and then lay it out on the table when it's time for guests to arrive. (Of course, a hot pot party can be fun for two or four people, too—just reduce the quantities of everything.)

Here's the basic anatomy of a hot pot dinner.

Pots for Hot Pot: They come in various shapes. My favorites have two compartments that easily hold both a spicy broth and a mild broth. You can find them in large Asian supermarkets or online.

Burners: The burner is usually a butane gas burner, but induction burners (and an extension cord) have become more commonplace. Using induction keeps you from constantly needing backup butane and prevents gas fumes from collecting in the house—and induction can get raging hot, too.

Broth: There are broth packets that come in many varieties (such as mushroom or tomato), and regional styles like spicy Szechuan and Chongqing. You can buy them ahead of time to have on hand, and all you have to do is pop them into hot water when you need them. They're compact and inexpensive, and I always keep a variety stored away in my pantry to use. You could theoretically use a homemade broth to do this but few Chinese households would take the time since they're so highly concentrated. Your time is better spent preparing for everything else in this situation.

Meats: Meats for hot pot should be sliced very thin. I use presliced frozen meats, usually beef, pork, or lamb. More recently, premium cuts of beef such as Wagyu have become available in some stores. Also consider using frozen boneless fish fillets, peeled and deveined shrimp, scallops, clams, and squid. Ask your butcher to slice for shabu-shabu if you can't find a store that sells meat like this regularly (although I should note that my Costco sells beef prepared in this way so keep an eye out).

Meatballs: Hot pot meatballs are some of the most popular things to cook. These feature a variety of meats; beef, pork, chicken, and fish are the most popular. I also like stuffed fish meatballs filled with roe.

Bean Curds and Gluten: Fried bean curd (aka tofu puffs) and fried gluten balls are delicious additions and give vegetarians a non-vegetable option at the table. You can find them in the refrigerated section where the tofu is in most Chinese markets. Whether or not you eat meat you should have these because nothing is better at soaking up the flavorful broth than tofu puffs and gluten.

Vegetables: Leafy greens like bok choy, cabbage, and yu choy are hot pot staples, but root vegetables like lotus and taro can be used as well. Lotus root is sweet and crisp no matter how long you cook it; cooked taro root has a creamy consistency, but keep an eye on that, as it can dissolve very quickly.

Sauces and Garnishes: I recommend putting many sauces and toppings on the table so people can make their own impromptu concoctions. Try any or all of the following: light soy sauce, dark soy sauce, Japanese soy sauce, sweet soy sauce (kecap manis), toasted sesame oil, minced garlic (raw or fried), fried shallots, minced fresh ginger, whole cilantro leaves (with tender stems is fine), Chinese sesame paste, toasted sesame oil, black bean paste, chili oil, chili crisp, sliced scallions, fish sauce, wasabi, broad bean paste, miso, doubanjiang, gochujang, sugar, pasteurized raw egg . . . and the list goes on.

244

Kung Food

Hong Kong Chicken and Waffles

Serves 4

Fried chicken

⅓ cup light soy sauce

⅓ cup Shaoxing wine

3 tablespoons sugar

2 tablespoons fish sauce

2 tablespoons kosher salt

1 tablespoon freshly ground
    black pepper

1 tablespoon freshly ground
    white pepper

1½ to 2 pounds boneless skin-on
    chicken thighs, cut into
    2-inch pieces

Neutral oil, for frying

2 cups potato starch

1 cup all-purpose flour

3 large eggs

Waffles

2 cups all-purpose flour

1½ cups sugar

2 tablespoons custard powder
    (available online)

1 tablespoon nonfat milk powder

1 tablespoon tapioca starch

2 teaspoons baking powder

4 large eggs

1½ cups whole milk

2 tablespoons vegetable oil, plus
    more for the waffle maker

2 teaspoons pure vanilla extract

Szechuan-Spiced Maple Syrup
    (page 48), for serving

Detroit's Breakfast House & Grill (now the Hudson Café) was where I first experienced the textural contrast of pillowy waffle and crunchy fried chicken skin, and the sweet-and-salty harmony of juicy dark meat chicken and a slick of maple syrup. The pairing was so satisfying that I fell into a ritual of having it delivered every Sunday morning after a late night out. It wasn't until many years later that I thought to try this dish in my own style using Hong Kong egg waffles (aka eggettes) and karaage (small bites of Japanese fried chicken). The combination— enhanced with the use of Szechuan peppercorns in the maple syrup and splashes of chili oil—became so popular that I was constantly encouraged to enter local fried chicken and waffle competitions (I never could bring myself to; I don't really enjoy competitive cooking). I particularly like tearing up the waffle into little individual pieces, then taking a fork and stabbing into one of those pieces, then stabbing a piece of chicken, then stabbing another piece of waffle. You now have a tiny and perfect fried chicken and waffle sandwich that you can eat plain or dunk into a ramekin of warm Szechuan-spiced maple syrup. The waffles are best made in a Hong Kong–style waffle/eggette maker, which they sell online in varying levels of quality. I understand it's a very specialized thing and of course you're free to use whatever waffle maker you already have, but the experience won't be quite the same without one. I've heard you can try to sub vanilla pudding mix for custard powder, but I've never tried it myself.

Marinate the chicken: In a large bowl, combine the soy sauce, wine, sugar, and fish sauce. Add the chicken, stir to coat, and refrigerate for 30 minutes. Remove the chicken from the marinade and transfer to a paper towel–lined plate, then return it to the refrigerator to air-dry for 30 minutes.

Fry the chicken: Preheat the oven to 200°F.

(recipe continues)

Fill a heavy saucepan, wok, or Dutch oven with neutral oil to a depth of 1½ inches and heat over medium-high heat to 350°F (or set your deep fryer to 350°F). Have a paper towel–lined baking sheet nearby.

Place the potato starch in a medium bowl and the flour in a second medium bowl. Mix 1 tablespoon of the salt, 1½ teaspoons of the black pepper, and 1½ teaspoons of the white pepper into each bowl. In a small bowl, beat the eggs.

Bread the chicken using a dry-wet-dry sequence: Working in batches, dredge the chicken in the flour mixture, then coat it in egg, then dredge it in the potato starch mixture. Gently place the breaded chicken in the hot oil (do not overcrowd) and fry until the chicken is golden and the internal temperature reaches 165°F, about 3 to 5 minutes. Use a slotted spoon or spider to transfer the chicken to the paper towels to drain, and repeat with the remaining chicken. Once you're finished with the whole batch of chicken, give it a quick double fry to really get them crispy, about 1 to 3 minutes. Set them all on a tray and keep the fried chicken warm in the oven until you're ready to serve it.

Make the waffles: In a medium bowl, combine the flour, sugar, custard powder, milk powder, tapioca starch, and baking powder. In a separate medium bowl, combine the eggs, milk, 2 tablespoons oil, and vanilla. Pour the wet ingredients into the dry ingredients and whisk just to combine.

Heat a waffle maker according to the manufacturer's instructions. Using a pastry brush, dab a bit of oil onto the plates of the waffle maker (every one I've come across has a nonstick coating, so avoid sprays, as those don't work well on nonstick surfaces). Add enough batter to fill the iron per the manufacturer's instructions and flip, if necessary (an eggette maker will require you to flip). Use the first waffle to gauge how much batter is needed to fill the iron going forward. Cook the waffles until golden and keep them warm in the oven until serving. Divide waffles and chicken evenly among serving plates and pass the syrup.

Beef and Broccoli Potpie

Serves 4

1 pound flank steak

¼ teaspoon baking soda

1½ teaspoons cornstarch

4 tablespoons neutral oil

1 teaspoon oyster sauce

4 cups chopped broccoli florets and stems (1- to 2-inch pieces)

1 sheet store-bought frozen puff pastry, thawed

1 tablespoon Shaoxing wine

1 teaspoon dark soy sauce

2½ tablespoons all-purpose flour

2 teaspoons freshly ground white pepper

1½ teaspoons sugar

1 teaspoon kosher salt

1 small yellow onion, halved and thinly sliced

½ cup English peas or frozen stir-fry medley (cubed carrots, peas, and corn; optional)

2 garlic cloves, grated

1 teaspoon grated fresh ginger

2 star anise pods

1 cup beef broth

1 large egg, beaten with 1 tablespoon water or milk, for the egg wash

After moving to Canada from Hong Kong, it was always such a treat when Mom brought home microwave chicken potpies, because anything that presented itself as strictly North American was wholly exotic to me and therefore special. The creaminess of the chicken with the sweetness of the suspiciously perfect cubes of carrots and the green-brown peas were so different from anything I normally ate at home. Though it was a simple lazy-day microwave meal for us as a family, it spawned my love for anything in pie form. This recipe pays homage to the quintessential Chinese American classic beef and broccoli—in a pie package.

Preheat the oven to 400°F.

Slice the beef with the grain into 1- to 2-inch-wide strips. Next, slice against the grain at a 45-degree angle to cut the beef into 1- to 2-inch squares with angled edges. Place the beef in a large bowl and add the baking soda and 3 tablespoons water. Massage the mixture into the beef. Add the cornstarch, 1 tablespoon of the oil, and the oyster sauce and toss to combine. Refrigerate for at least 30 minutes and up to 4 hours.

Spread the broccoli over a baking sheet and toss with 1 tablespoon of the oil. Roast for 20 minutes, or until the broccoli florets have a little char, turning once halfway through. Remove the pan from the oven and set aside; reduce the oven temperature to 350°F.

Line a baking sheet with parchment paper. Set the puff pastry on a cutting board and trim it to a circle that will fit on top of a 10- or 12-inch oven-safe skillet (cast iron is ideal; the pastry will rest on top of the filling, so it should match the width of your skillet at the top of the pan rather than the bottom). Set the pastry on the parchment-lined baking sheet and refrigerate.

(recipe continues)

In a small bowl, combine the wine and soy sauce. In a separate small bowl, combine the flour, white pepper, sugar, and salt. Set both bowls aside.

In a 10- to 12-inch oven-safe sauté pan (cast iron is ideal), heat 1 tablespoon of the oil over medium-high heat. Add the beef and cook until browned on all sides, about 5 to 7 minutes. Transfer the meat to a plate and set aside. Add the remaining 1 tablespoon oil to the pan, then add the onion and peas (if using) and cook, stirring, until the onion becomes translucent, about 3 minutes. Add the garlic and ginger and cook for 30 seconds, just until fragrant, then add the vegetable mixture to the plate with the beef.

Pour the wine mixture into the empty pan and use a wooden spoon to scrape up any browned bits from the bottom, then stir in the flour mixture. Add the star anise and the broth to the pan as you stir. The liquid should thicken to a gravy consistency after a couple of minutes.

Use a fork to remove the star anise, if you insist (I generally leave whole spices in my food and eat around them). Remove the pastry from the refrigerator and lay it on top of the filling in the skillet—don't seal or dock it, because you want the pastry to rise high. Brush with the egg wash and place the potpie in the oven. Bake for 20 minutes, or until the crust is golden. Remove from the oven and serve hot.

Kung Fu Means "With Effort"

Kung Food

Dan Dan Lasagna

Serves 4

Lasagna

Kosher salt
16 ounces lasagna noodles
(preferably the curly edged
kind)
2 tablespoons unsalted butter
1 (15-ounce) ricotta cheese
16 ounces mozzarella cheese or
Wisconsin Brick, grated
¼ cup grated Parmesan or
Manchego cheese, or
crumbled goat cheese

Dan dan sauce

1 tablespoon neutral oil
1½ pounds ground pork
1 medium white or yellow onion,
diced
8 garlic cloves, grated
1 tablespoon grated fresh ginger
1 tablespoon Szechuan
peppercorns
2 teaspoons ground cumin
2 tablespoons chopped dried
Szechuan chilies or other hot
red chilies
¼ cup ya cai (preserved mustard
greens)
¼ cup water or store-bought
chicken broth

When I was little, I would sometimes ask for lasagna minutes before dinnertime. Of course, we had only Stouffer's lasagna at home, and it was still in the freezer when I asked, so after a few thwarted efforts, I learned about the necessity of thinking ahead for dinner.

This cheesy and indulgent lasagna is how I'm bringing my love for that childhood favorite into my tastes as an adult. The sweetness of Stouffer's tomato sauce is replaced with a tingly and spicy dan dan noodle–inspired mixture that better suits my present-day need for spice. Feel free to get a little freaky and try this with ground lamb instead of ground pork; use an extra teaspoon of cumin if you do.

Make the lasagna: Bring a large pot of salted water to a boil over high heat. Add the lasagna noodles and cook for a minute or so less than the package instructions indicate (they'll continue to cook in the oven). Drain, rinse with cold water, and toss with the butter to prevent sticking.

In a large bowl, mix the ricotta with 1 teaspoon salt. Stir in the mozzarella and the Parmesan and set aside.

Make the dan dan sauce: In a large sauté pan, heat the oil over medium-high heat. Add the ground pork and cook, stirring often to break it up into smaller pieces, until browned and mostly cooked through, about 5 to 8 minutes. Transfer to a bowl.

Return the pan to medium-high heat and add the onion, garlic, ginger, Szechuan pepper, cumin, dried chilies, and ya cai. Cook, stirring often, until the onion is translucent, about 3 minutes. Add the water or broth, soy sauce, tomatoes with their juices, and cornstarch and stir to mix well. Return the pork to the pan and use your spoon to further break down the pieces of pork for an even consistency.

(recipe and ingredients continue)

251

¾ teaspoon light soy sauce or
Tomato Soy Sauce (page 52)
1 (28-ounce) can whole peeled
San Marzano tomatoes,
with their juices, blended or
mashed
1 tablespoon cornstarch

Neutral oil, for greasing
Basic Chili Oil (page 44)
Five-Spice Powder (page 59)

Reduce the heat to low and cook until the loose liquid has evaporated as much as possible, and you have a very thick and uniform meat sauce. (The sauce can be cooled and stored in an airtight container in the refrigerator for up to 3 days.)

Preheat the oven to 350°F. Grease the bottom and sides of a 9 by 13-inch casserole dish with an oiled paper towel.

Spoon a very thin layer of meat sauce across the bottom of the oiled dish. Place a layer of noodles (usually 3 or 4) side by side over the sauce and then add one-quarter of the cheese mixture. Follow with another noodle layer, one-third of the remaining meat sauce, and one-third of the remaining cheese. Then drizzle with a little chili oil (about 1 tablespoon) and add a few dashes of five-spice powder (about ½ teaspoon). Repeat two more times, until you have four layers of noodles, finishing with the last of the cheese on top. Sprinkle with more chili oil and five-spice.

Bake for 30 to 45 minutes, until the lasagna is bubbling and the cheese layer on top begins to brown. Remove from the oven and set aside to cool and settle for 20 minutes before slicing and serving.

Thunder Bay Bon Bons
(Ribs) with B-Z 骨 Sauce

Serves 4

Ribs

3½ to 4 pounds pork spareribs,
    cut into individual ribs
1 tablespoon light soy sauce
2 teaspoons dark soy sauce
1 tablespoon Five-Spice Powder
    (page 59)
2 teaspoons sugar
1 teaspoon MSG

Sauce

¾ cup dark soy sauce
¼ cup light soy sauce
½ cup Shaoxing wine
2 thumb-size pieces fresh ginger,
    peeled and thinly sliced
3 star anise pods
2 cinnamon sticks
1 black cardamom pod, cracked
1 cup brown sugar

Frying

Neutral oil
2 cups cornstarch or potato
    starch
1 tablespoon Five-Spice
    Powder (page 59), or use
    store-bought
2 teaspoons kosher salt
1 teaspoon freshly ground white
    pepper
2 large eggs

My mom used to take me to this Chinese restaurant in downtown Toronto, where the only two dishes that stuck in my mind were the bok choy and a dish I called "B-Z 骨." The reason I remember the bok choy was because while eating it, I found a dead caterpillar nestled in the leaves, which scarred me for life and made me averse to what had been my favorite vegetable. The latter was a dish of pork ribs that I remember because it was so tasty. Indeed, B-Z 骨 wasn't even the name of the dish; that was what I called it. My mom would apologetically order it by this name and the server had to figure out what the hell she was talking about. I never had them again outside of that one restaurant, and she never could remember what they were actually called.

In my quest to find those ribs, I came across Thunder Bay Bon Bons. By their description as crispy-fried spareribs, they seemed to be what I remembered, except with the addition of that sweet and savory sauce. The ribs themselves were simple enough, marinated in five-spice and MSG and then fried, so I tossed them in my best improvisation of the sticky sauce, and I honestly think I managed to get it. Accurate or not, it's damn delicious.

Marinate the ribs: Put the ribs in a large (gallon-size) freezer bag and add the light soy sauce, dark soy sauce, five-spice, sugar, and MSG. Seal the bag and slosh it around so everything mixes and coats the ribs. Marinate in the refrigerator for at least 1 hour but no longer than 3 hours.

Make the sauce: In a small saucepan, combine the dark and light soy sauce, wine, ginger, 1 cup water, star anise, cinnamon, and cardamom and bring to a simmer over medium heat. Simmer until fragrant, about 25 minutes. Remove the spices before adding the sugar, reduce the heat to low, and stir until a syrup forms, 10 to 15 minutes. Remove from the heat; the sauce will continue to thicken as it cools.

(recipe continues)

Kung Fu Means "With Effort"

Fry the ribs: Fill a wok or Dutch oven with oil to a depth of at least 4 inches and heat over medium-high heat to 350°F. Set a large wire rack over a baking sheet and have it nearby.

In a large bowl, mix the cornstarch, five-spice, salt, and white pepper, then spread the mixture over a large plate. Beat the eggs in a large bowl.

Remove the ribs from the marinade and use paper towels to pat dry, then add them to the bowl with the eggs and turn so they are lightly coated on both sides. Working with one at a time, let the excess egg drip off, then toss the rib in the cornstarch mixture and set it on the rack. Each rib should have a thick enough coating of cornstarch that no meat is visible.

Working in batches, add the ribs to the hot oil and fry for about 5 minutes, until golden brown, keeping an eye on the temperature of the oil to keep it at 350°F. Use tongs to transfer the ribs to the rack and fry the next batch.

While the ribs are cooking, warm the sauce over low heat (at room temperature, it's usually too thick to easily coat the ribs).

When ready to serve, either put the fried ribs in a large bowl and toss with just enough sauce to coat or use a spoon to drizzle over the ribs to taste (any leftover sauce can be refrigerated in an airtight container for up to 2 weeks and used with rice or noodles). Transfer to a serving dish and serve.

Kung Fu Means "With Effort"

Kung Food

Steamed Fish

Serves 4 to 6

2 thumb-size pieces fresh
    ginger, peeled and julienned
8 scallions, thinly sliced
2 (1½- to 2-pound) whole red
    snapper or other white-
    fleshed fish, scaled and
    gutted
½ cup light soy sauce
1 tablespoon sugar
¼ cup neutral oil
1 cup packed fresh cilantro
    leaves
Steamed rice, for serving

I know serving a whole fish is said to have many celebratory implications in Chinese culture, but as a third-culture kid, a lot of its meaning and significance was lost to me. It's something about prosperity; I know that much. Either way, steamed fish is delicious. The best kinds of fish to use for this dish are white-fleshed (not tuna or salmon) and lean (not mackerel, trout, or herring). Red snapper, branzino, tilapia, and cod are all fine staples for steaming, but also give black sea bass, pompano, and grouper a try if you have a good source for them. This style is more of a Cantonese preparation and is savory, sweet, and mild. The variation, which calls for duo jiao (chopped fermented chilies; see page 55) is very loosely based on more of a Hunan-style preparation.

Set up a steamer: If using a wok (recommended), set a plate holder or a heat-safe medium bowl or other heat-safe object inside the wok to use as a pedestal. Find a dish large enough to accommodate the fish in a single layer (you should still be able to easily cover the wok with a lid and have a tight seal). Add water to the bottom of the wok and heat over high heat. (Alternatively, you may steam the fish in a very large steamer basket—large enough that the fish lie flat—and then move the fish to another pan to finish the flash-frying process.)

Place half the ginger and half the scallions on the dish you'll use for the fish and then place the fish on top. In a small bowl, stir together the soy sauce and sugar until the sugar dissolves. When the water in the wok is simmering, carefully set the dish with the fish on the pedestal and pour ¼ cup of the soy sauce mixture on top of the fish. Cover the wok and steam until the fish is just cooked through, about 15 minutes. (To check doneness with skin-on fish, cut into the thickest part of the fish with the tip of a paring knife and see if the meat separates easily from the bones.)

(recipe continues)

While the fish is steaming, in a small saucepan, heat the oil over low heat until it is very hot, with bubbles forming around the edge, but not smoking (a thermometer should read between 375° and 400°F).

Turn off the heat under the wok and carefully uncover it, opening the wok lid away from you (so the steam doesn't rise into your face). Remove the plate with the fish from the wok and place it on a serving platter. Pour the liquid out of the steamer and take out the aromatics. Top the fish with the remaining ¼ cup soy sauce mixture, half the cilantro, and the remaining ginger. (Removing the old water and the old aromatics takes out much of the fishy taste, and replacing with fresh aromatics and a splash of hot oil addresses a fresh fragrance to the fish.)

Pour the hot oil over the aromatics, using just enough to lightly coat the fish and herbs (you may not need to use all the oil). Top with the remaining cilantro and scallions and serve immediately with rice.

For an alternate, spicier version, follow the instructions on page 257, but before pouring the soy sauce mixture over the fish, instead cover it with 1 cup Duo Jiao (page 55), then steam as directed. Once the fish is cooked through, finish as instructed with the hot oil and aromatics.

Char Siu Baby Back Ribs

Serves 4

Char siu sauce

1 cup honey
1 cup Shaoxing wine
½ cup hoisin sauce
¼ cup oyster sauce
2 tablespoons Chinese red
   vinegar
1½ teaspoons light soy sauce
1½ teaspoons dark soy sauce
2 cubes red fermented tofu
2 teaspoons freshly ground
   white pepper
1½ teaspoons freshly ground
   black pepper
1 tablespoon ground red
   yeast rice

Ribs

1 cup kosher salt
1 cup sugar
1 (2½- to 3-pound) rack baby
   back pork ribs
2 tablespoons Five-Spice
   Powder (page 59), or use
   store-bought
2 tablespoons ground cumin
1 tablespoon freshly ground
   white pepper
1 tablespoon freshly ground
   black pepper
1 tablespoon ground ginger
1 teaspoon cayenne pepper
Neutral oil (optional)

I've never understood why you don't see Cantonese-style BBQ sauces used more like Western barbecue sauce—seems like it should work on paper, since Western barbecue sauce is typically (as traditional American barbecue) just as savory and sweet as the Chinese version. The main difference between the two is how you get to savory/sweet (spices, soy sauce, fermented bean curd . . .). If you're using a grill, the added benefit of charcoal smoke adds further richness to the overall product, which I highly recommend. The red coloring in this recipe comes from two sources: red fermented bean curd and red yeast rice. Both add a richness to the flavor of the ribs that red food coloring cannot replicate, and both are musts for this recipe—you can find them at Chinese grocery stores and online. Red yeast rice is used a lot in Chinese medicine to help with blood circulation and is also found in some Peking duck and red vinegar recipes. Fermented bean curd is used as a savory, sometimes tangy, addition to sauces and is also eaten as an accompaniment to rice. Sometimes it's referred to as "Chinese cheese" because of its fantastic funkiness.

Make the char siu sauce: In a large saucepan, combine the honey, wine, hoisin, oyster sauce, vinegar, light soy sauce, dark soy sauce, tofu, white pepper, black pepper, and red yeast rice and whisk to combine. Cook over medium heat—smoosh the cubes of fermented red tofu with a fork to help them dissolve as the sauce cooks—for 10 to 15 minutes, until the sauce has a thick, pourable consistency. Remove from the heat and let cool to room temperature. (The cooled sauce can be stored in the refrigerator, tightly covered, for up to 1 week.)

Brine the ribs: In a very large bowl or stockpot, combine the salt and sugar with 1 gallon water and stir to dissolve. Place the ribs in the liquid and brine in the refrigerator for at least 1 hour and up to 2 hours.

(recipe continues)

259

Meanwhile, in a small bowl, combine the five-spice, cumin, white pepper, black pepper, ginger, and cayenne to make a rub. Remove the ribs from the brine and pat them dry. Cover the ribs with the rub on all sides, then refrigerate for at least 30 minutes or up to 6 hours, if you want to plan ahead.

Grill the ribs: Heat a grill to 350°F and oil the grill grates. Place the ribs on the grill meat-side up, close the lid, and then open the vent so that the temperature starts dropping. Keeping the grill at 250°F, cook the ribs, flipping them every 30 minutes, for about 2 hours, until the meat is tender (cut a piece off with a knife to check).

Bake the ribs: Preheat the oven to 400°F. Place the ribs on a wire rack meat-side down and set the rack on a baking sheet. Place in the oven, then immediately reduce the oven temperature to 250°F. For tender meat that stays on the bone, cook the ribs for 2 hours total, flipping them once midway through. For off-the-bone ribs, cover the ribs with aluminum foil and cook for an additional hour.

Whether you're grilling or baking the ribs, during the last 30 minutes of cooking, brush both sides of the rack with the char siu sauce.

Cut the rack into individual ribs and serve right from the cutting board, with more sauce alongside.

Kung Fu Means "With Effort"

Feijoada "Chinêsa"

Serves 6

3 unsmoked pork trotters,
  quartered by your butcher
2 unsmoked pork ribs, quartered
  by your butcher
2 pig tails, split (optional)
2 pork tongues (optional)
¼ cup aniseed
8 ounces bacon, roughly
  chopped
12 garlic cloves, roughly
  chopped
1 white or yellow onion, roughly
  chopped
1 tablespoon Cumin-Based
  Five-Spice Powder
  (page 60)
3 cups dry white wine (or
  store-bought chicken broth,
  if avoiding alcohol)
1 pound dried black beans
4 bay leaves
6 Chinese sausages, sliced on an
  angle ½ inch thick
1 strip lap yuk (Chinese cured
  pork belly; see Note,
  page 171), cut into 1-inch
  pieces
1 orange, halved
Steamed rice, for serving
Cooked Farofa, for serving

My mom spent a bit of time in Goiana, Brazil, when she was growing up. In fact, a whole section of her side of the family lives in Brazil, so it's not all that surprising that she'd occasionally fix us up a batch of feijoada. It was also one of the first things she taught me how to make when I was living on my own in my first apartment in Detroit. She didn't so much teach me a recipe as show me the process, so I rarely paid much attention to the ingredient measurements (who am I kidding—I still don't pay attention to measurements). It was this dish—to the surprise of a few Detroiters—that I started serving at some of my first neighborhood pop-ups. One time, finding myself all prepped and ready and having forgotten the Calabrese sausage that was traditionally used, I decided to add Chinese sausage, Jinhua ham, and cured pork belly, just to see what would happen. It proved to be a hit with the neighbors, but especially with the Brazilian guests who really appreciated the sweetness of the sausage and pork belly. Happy accidents, as it were.

Farofa is a coarse cassava flour commonly used as a garnish in Brazil. You can buy raw farofa (called manioc flour; make sure you buy coarse ground and not fine) and toast it with butter in a skillet until golden brown, but there is also ready-to-serve farofa available in some South American groceries and online.

In a stockpot or large Dutch oven, combine the trotters, ribs, tails and tongues (if using), and aniseed. Add enough water to cover by 2 inches and bring to a boil over high heat. Reduce the heat to medium and cook for 10 minutes. Use a slotted spoon to remove the tongues and place them on a cutting board. Remove the membrane from the tongues and discard; set the tongues aside. Remove the ribs and set them aside with the tongues. Cook the trotters for 35 minutes more, then drain the offal and rinse off all the aniseed.

Clean the pot and add the bacon. Slowly cook over medium heat for about 5 minutes, until it has rendered sufficient fat to cook the aromatics. Add the garlic and onion and cook, stirring occasionally, till fragrant and translucent, about 3 minutes. Add the five-spice and toast it in the bacon fat until the spices are aromatic, then add the wine and stir to deglaze the pot. Simmer for 3 minutes, then add the beans. Return the trotters, ribs, tails, and tongues to the pot, then add the bay leaves, sausages, lap yuk, and half of the orange. Add 6 quarts (24 cups) water and bring to a boil over high heat. Reduce the heat to maintain a simmer, cover, and cook until the beans are completely soft, about 2 hours, checking the pot occasionally after the first hour of cooking and topping off with water if needed.

Turn off the heat, uncover, and remove all the meats and sausages from the pot, and remove the bay leaves. Set aside to cool, then remove all the flesh from the bones of the trotters and ribs and slice the tongues into bite-size pieces before putting it all back in the pot and simmering again, uncovered, for 20 minutes to 1 hour more, until the liquid has reduced to the consistency of a stew. My mom likes to mash the beans a little before putting all the meat back in so it gets *really* thick, while I make mine a little thinner, like a stew. Serve with a side of rice, farofa, and slices from the other half of the orange.

Kung Fu Means "With Effort"

Kung Food

Shanghainese Smoked Fish Tacos

Serves 8

1 whole smoked whitefish
(about 2 pounds, picked), or
1¾ pounds smoked boneless
whitefish fillets
½ cup lightly packed light brown
sugar
½ cup Shaoxing wine
¼ cup light soy sauce
¼ cup oyster sauce
2 tablespoons dark soy sauce
2 thumb-size pieces fresh
ginger, peeled and thinly
sliced (about ¼ cup)
3 star anise pods
2 slivers Chinese licorice root
(see Note, page 43)
2 bay leaves
1 black cardamom pod, cracked
2 tablespoons neutral oil
8 corn tortillas
Fish Taco Slaw (recipe follows)

The classic dish of Shanghainese smoked fish isn't actually smoked; the fish is fried in oil and then soaked in a pungent sweet-and-salty sauce. But for this recipe, I did use a whole smoked whitefish, which I found at my farmers' market—it's also readily available at Jewish delis, some seafood markets, and online (you can ask a fishmonger to fillet it for you). Use boneless fillets if you can find them, but whole smoked whitefish is much more widely available. The smoky flavor adds its own depth to the Shanghainese preparation of quick-frying in oil. Combined with the Shanghainese-inspired sauce and creamy slaw, it works perfectly folded into a hot corn tortilla for a somewhat California-style fish taco.

Remove the bones from the fish (this might be easy or more surgical, depending on the way it was prepared). Cut or tear the fish into 8 pieces and set aside. You can also pick the fish into small flakes and assemble them into piles if that's easier.

In a small saucepan, combine the brown sugar, wine, light soy sauce, oyster sauce, dark soy sauce, ginger, star anise, licorice root, bay leaves, and cardamom. Bring to a simmer over medium-low heat, then simmer for 30 minutes, until thick and syrupy. Strain (discard the solids) and set aside.

In a large sauté pan, heat the oil over medium-high heat. Fry the fish on both sides until golden brown and warmed through, about 2 minutes per side. Add just enough sauce to the pan to lightly coat the fish, toss, and heat through. (The extra sauce will keep in an airtight container in the fridge for at least 2 weeks.)

Heat the corn tortillas according to the package directions or personal preference (the easiest way to do this is in a skillet over medium heat until pliable). Make tacos by stuffing the tortillas with fish and topping them with slaw.

(recipe continues)

Kung Fu Means "With Effort"

Fish Taco Slaw

2 tablespoons mayonnaise (preferably Kewpie)
2 tablespoons fresh lime juice
2 garlic cloves, grated
½ teaspoon kosher salt
¼ teaspoon freshly ground white pepper
½ medium head red or white cabbage, shredded
   (about 4 cups)
4 scallions, thinly sliced
2 large carrots, grated (about 1 cup)
½ cup packed fresh cilantro leaves
2 jalapeños, halved, seeded, and minced

In a large bowl, mix the mayonnaise, lime juice,
garlic, salt, and white pepper until smooth. Add the
cabbage, scallions, carrots, cilantro, and jalapeños
and toss with your hands until well combined.
Store in the refrigerator, tightly covered, for up
to 2 days.

My old roommate Alejandro would tell me to look for the tortillas with a lady on the label because that's usually the good one. I said the same thing to him when I sent him out for Chinese Chili Crisp.

Kung Fu Means "With Effort"

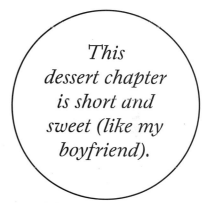

This dessert chapter is short and sweet (like my boyfriend).

Desserts and a Drink

Kung Food

Glam Trash Cake Rangoons

Makes 12 rangoons

4 Hostess Ding Dongs (I'm
  sorry)
¼ cup strawberry Calpico
  (No, seriously, you guys. I'm
  really sorry.)
1 (8-ounce) block cream cheese,
  at room temperature
1 hot dog (Please don't leave.
  I swear I'm a professional.),
  minced
Honey, for garnish
Fruity Pebbles (Wait. Where are
  you going?), for garnish
12 wonton wrappers
Neutral oil, for frying

A certain production company filmed me on behalf of a particular gastronomic network to "test my range for TV," putting me in a situation where they brought a bunch of ingredients completely out of my control or knowledge and told me to make food out of them. What I prepared was an embarrassingly tasty dessert rangoon that I'm sharing with you because sharing is how we heal from trauma. If you haven't come across Calpico before, it's kind of like a yogurt drink, and for this challenge they handed me the strawberry version. I'm going to say right now that strawberry is not my favorite. On its own, I don't really care for it, but in the rangoon, it gives the cake filling an almost strawberry cheesecake quality. It's easy to find at Japanese and other Asian groceries.

In a food processor, combine the Ding Dongs, Calpico, and cream cheese and process to combine. Use a rubber spatula to transfer the mixture to a medium bowl. This will be the filling.

Set a small nonstick skillet over medium heat. Add the hot dog to the pan and fry until you have tiny crispy little bits, almost like bacon bits. Set aside. Put the honey and Fruity Pebbles in two separate small bowls and set aside.

Set a small bowl of water on your work surface. Place the wonton wrappers on a cutting board and use a small spoon to add about 2 teaspoons of the filling to the center of each wrapper.

This is the simplest way to fold, rangoon-style: Dip a finger into the water and moisten the edges of the wrapper, then bring each corner to the center, pressing the seams together so it makes a square shape with the seams forming four lines that radiate from the center. Repeat with the remaining rangoons. Take care to seal these very well, because the cake filling can easily escape a poorly sealed rangoon, leaving you with burnt cake oil and an empty wonton.

(recipe continues)

271

Deep-fry according to the directions on page 146, though fry for only about 3 minutes, until lightly golden, since nothing in the filling needs to cook. Take care to cook around 300°F and be gentle. Use a slotted spoon or spider to transfer the rangoons to a paper towel–lined baking sheet or plate to cool very slightly.

As soon as you can touch the rangoons without burning your fingers, dip each into the honey and then into the Fruity Pebbles to make it pretty. Top each rangoon with one or two of the wiener bits. Vaya con Dios.

It was at this photo shoot where I learned that feigned enthusiasm is not something I can do.

272

Five-Spice Rolls
with Milk Tea Glaze

Makes 7 to 8 large rolls

Dough

Neutral oil, for greasing
¾ cup whole milk
1 (¼-ounce) packet rapid-rise
 yeast (2¼ teaspoons)
4¼ cups bread flour
½ cup cornstarch
½ cup granulated sugar
1½ teaspoons kosher salt
3 large eggs, at room
 temperature
12 tablespoons (1½ sticks)
 unsalted butter, cut into
 12 pieces, at room
 temperature

Filling

1½ cups light brown sugar
1 tablespoon ground cinnamon
1 tablespoon ground Szechuan
 pepper
2 teaspoons ground cardamom
 seeds (green or black)
1½ teaspoons ground ginger
1 star anise pod, ground
Kosher salt
2 tablespoons unsalted butter,
 at room temperature

When we lived in Detroit's Eastern Market neighborhood, my boyfriend and I had a Saturday morning ritual where we'd catch the neighborhood farmers' market before the crowds came. There was a Mennonite stall where the ladies had cakes, pies, cookies, and all other kinds of sweets. He always bought a half dozen oatmeal cream pies for himself to eat during the week, but we both enjoyed their cinnamon rolls, tall and proud, turned warm and gooey after a quick minute in the microwave. Those will be mornings I cherish as one of the things we did together that is the inspiration for these sweet and sticky rolls.

Make the dough: Grease a medium bowl with oil. In a pot or using the microwave, heat the milk, then let it cool to between 100° and 110°F (it should feel just warm to the touch, not hot). Add the yeast and stir until the yeast dissolves and starts to bubble.

In the bowl of a stand mixer fitted with the dough hook, combine the flour, cornstarch, granulated sugar, and salt and mix until combined. With the mixer running on low speed, slowly add the milk-yeast mixture until it comes together, about a minute, then add the eggs one at a time until fully incorporated.

Increase the speed to medium and add the butter pieces, waiting for each to be fully incorporated before adding the next. Mix the dough until it's smooth and doesn't stick to the bowl, 8 to 10 minutes more.

Place the dough on a clean surface and knead by hand until it forms a smooth, round ball. Transfer the dough to the greased bowl and cover with plastic wrap. Place the bowl in a warm part of the kitchen (above the fridge, for example) and let rise until doubled in size, about 2 hours.

273

(recipe and ingredients continue)

Glaze

1½ cups milk
¼ cup loose-leaf Assam or Irish breakfast tea (you can take this from tea bags)
¼ cup loose-leaf Pu-erh tea
3 cups confectioners' sugar
1 teaspoon pure vanilla extract
Kosher salt

While the dough rests, prepare the filling: In a medium bowl, combine the brown sugar, cinnamon, Szechuan pepper, cardamom, ginger, star anise, and a pinch of salt and set aside.

Line a large (at least 10-inch-diameter) ovenproof skillet with parchment paper. Transfer the dough to a clean surface and roll it out into an 18-inch square. Using fingers or a brush, spread the butter over the dough and evenly sprinkle the buttered dough with the spice mixture. Roll the dough into a tight cylinder and pinch where the dough sheet ends so that it no longer has an edge or a seam. Cut the cylinder crosswise into 8 even pieces using nonflavored dental floss or a very sharp bread knife. Transfer them cut-side up to the prepared skillet, cover with plastic wrap, and set aside to rise for 1 hour.

Preheat the oven to 350°F. Bake until deep and golden brown, about 35 to 45 minutes.

While the buns cook, make the glaze: In a medium saucepan, combine the milk and both the Assam and Pu-erh tea leaves. Bring to a simmer over medium heat, then turn off the heat and let steep for 30 minutes. Strain the milk into a small bowl. Put the confectioners' sugar in a large bowl and whisk in ¼ cup of the milk mixture until it creates a thick paste, adding more if necessary so the sugar dissolves into the liquid. Whisk in the vanilla and a pinch of salt. Add a little more of the milk mixture, if necessary, to create a glaze that is thick but can still be drizzled from a spoon without clumping.

Transfer the buns to a wire rack and drizzle with the glaze; allow the glaze to cool and set before adding another layer. Alternatively, leave the buns in the skillet and cover with the glaze. Everything looks better in a skillet.

275

Kung Food

Chile Chipotle Mango Pudding

Serves 4

3 very ripe (even overripe) mangoes
1 cup sugar
4 sheets gelatin, or 1 (¼-ounce) packet granulated gelatin (about 2½ teaspoons), or 1 teaspoon agar powder (to make it vegan)
1 cup boiling water
½ teaspoon ground chipotle chile
6 tablespoons evaporated milk (or coconut cream, to make it vegan)
1 tablespoon Tajín seasoning
1 lime, cut into wedges (optional)

Chinese desserts have a way of living as a constant in your memory. The preparations are so universal that they taste reliably the same no matter where you eat them. Ask someone from Hong Kong and another person from San Francisco, Sydney, Toronto, or London to describe a dim sum mango pudding, and all will likely have similar experiences to report. That's great, because it's a near-perfect dessert. However, I wanted to try to create something with more of an American signature and was inspired by how my Mexican neighbors combine the flavors of chile and mango. You'll also find vegan substitutes here, because why not.

Slice a thin bit off the bottom of a mango so you can easily stand it upright. Cut the mango vertically along the pit to remove the two meaty pieces on either side. Use a spoon to scoop as much flesh as possible from the skin and place it in a food processor or blender. Repeat with the other mangoes and then process or blend the flesh to a smooth purée. Measure 2 cups of the purée and set aside (eat or discard any leftover purée).

Place the sugar in a large heat-safe bowl.

Add the gelatin to the boiling water and soak until completely dissolved. Pour the hot liquid over the sugar and stir until the sugar dissolves. Add the mango purée, chipotle, and evaporated milk and whisk to combine.

Divide the pudding among four 6- to 8-ounce ramekins. Cover with plastic wrap and refrigerate until solid, at least 3 hours or up to 3 days. Before serving, top with a dusting of Tajín and an optional squeeze of lime.

Vanilla Rooibos Milk Tea

Makes 4 cups

½ cup black tea leaves
  (preferably Assam or Irish
  breakfast)
2 tablespoons Pu-erh tea leaves
2 tablespoons rooibos tea leaves
½ teaspoon pure vanilla extract
Sweetened condensed milk

Milk tea is an icon, a legend, and the moment. It's a classic drink from Hong Kong's teahouses: a mix of Chinese tea blends, usually a closely kept secret (and a bit different from shop to shop), mixed with milk and sugar (or condensed milk) and served either hot or cold. It's a common breakfast accompaniment and midafternoon pick-me-up. After many attempts at finding my perfect tea leaf combination for milk tea, I've settled on a blend of Assam or Irish breakfast, Pu-erh, and rooibos, with a drop of vanilla. This tea is equally good hot or iced—or poured over boba.

Place all three tea varieties in a heatproof bowl or large teapot with a strainer. In a saucepan or kettle, bring 5 cups water to a boil over high heat. Pour the boiling water over the tea leaves, cover, and steep for 6 minutes. At this stage, the tea will be too strong to drink on its own.

Strain the tea into a bowl (discard the solids) and stir in the vanilla. The milk tea base can be refrigerated in a tightly covered container for up to 2 weeks; reheat before adding condensed milk.

To serve, fill a glass three-quarters of the way and add condensed milk to sweeten to taste. Serve hot or over ice.

Desserts and a Drink

Acknowledgments

I put off writing this up until the very last minute because it's a sign that the process is finally coming to an end. It feels like that moment before you jump into a freezing cold pool. You're ready but also not ready to make it happen. When I was little I used to think to myself, "Oh well, here we go," every time before making that jump into the water as a way of telling myself the discomfort will be quick to pass and it isn't a big deal. It always got me in the water, whether I was ready for it or not. I never felt fully ready no matter how long I stood there at the edge of the pool.

Oh well. Here we go.

Erik Kim and Rick Martinez: Without the two of you (for thinking I had something important to say to some people who were important, and bringing me onto that random quarantine Zoom call to talk about my philosophy on food), none of this would have happened. You two weren't so much the push that set the wheels in motion as much as the creators of the world where the wheels existed in the first place. You were both so quick with kind advice throughout this process. I'm so lucky to know the both of you.

To Raquel Pelzel who saw something in my five minutes of rambling and followed up with the email that would change my life forever. I never thought a book was something that would ever be possible for me and you saw things differently. Look at that: You were right.

To Katherine Cowles who held my hand throughout the journey and went above and beyond with your effort in finding me the help I needed and continuing to look when that help would fall through. Your experience and wisdom helped me through what was otherwise an isolating process—none of this would have survived without your guidance.

Bianca Cruz for keeping it all the f*** together. For herding all the cats. And for the friendly IG messages, if only to let me know you're there if I needed someone.

Andy Baraghani: You're so g**d*** stylish, we only talked about this book for maybe half an hour total and it's so so so much sexier as a result.

Josh Cohen and Brian Sokolik: Thank you for making sure the rest of my life was sorted throughout this process. Keeping the other parts in focus and always reminding me that you guys were there if I really needed help.

Charlie Hillman and Grace Owens-Stively: For the reminders, for the organization, and especially for all the really warm and friendly communication of all these things. I'm so grateful to you both.

Nils Bernstein, thank you for dealing with the mess that is my writing and turning this jumble of gross inexperience into an actual book; you're the foundation that this is all built on.

Su Barber: We only needed like two forty-five minute meetings before you went off designing the most beautiful pages I'd ever seen in a cookbook. I really said, "color, style, and disco." And you made that into this.

Marysarah Quinn: For your guidance and hard work along with Su for making this beautiful book possible, and for your eye and guidance during the shoot. We know we did something right whenever you said something was beautiful.

Elizabeth Bossin, Sara Dickerman, Grace Rosanova, and Danielle DeLott: For translating the chicken scratch that only made sense to me into fully realized recipes. I've made recipes for my entire professional life but never once written one with the intention that it would be read by anyone other than me. Things would have been so lost without you all.

Johnny Miller: The photographs speak for themselves. You were such a creative joy to work with. The playfulness of those shoot days resulted in something more grand than I could have ever hoped for.

Rebecca Jurkevich: Thank you for keeping us all together, organized, and making sure it was all executed. You made food that I thought could only be comforting and look humble into the most beautiful but still true representations of themselves.

Cybelle Tondu and Joe Rumi: For your incredibly skilled hands in the kitchen, unmatched hard work in making the shoot possible, and immaculate taste in music.

Sarah Smart: Thank you for finding every texture, every tool, and every color, for us to play with. For literally setting the stage so the rest of it could shine.

To the production team at Clarkson Potter for compiling all of this mess into the thing we hold now.

To Joanne and Dylan who refused to see anything but the best in me.

To Kim, because we both know *gestures to myself and everything around me*—a lot of this is your fault.

To Jonathon, would you perhaps consider marrying me?

Index

Note: Page references in *italics* indicate photographs.

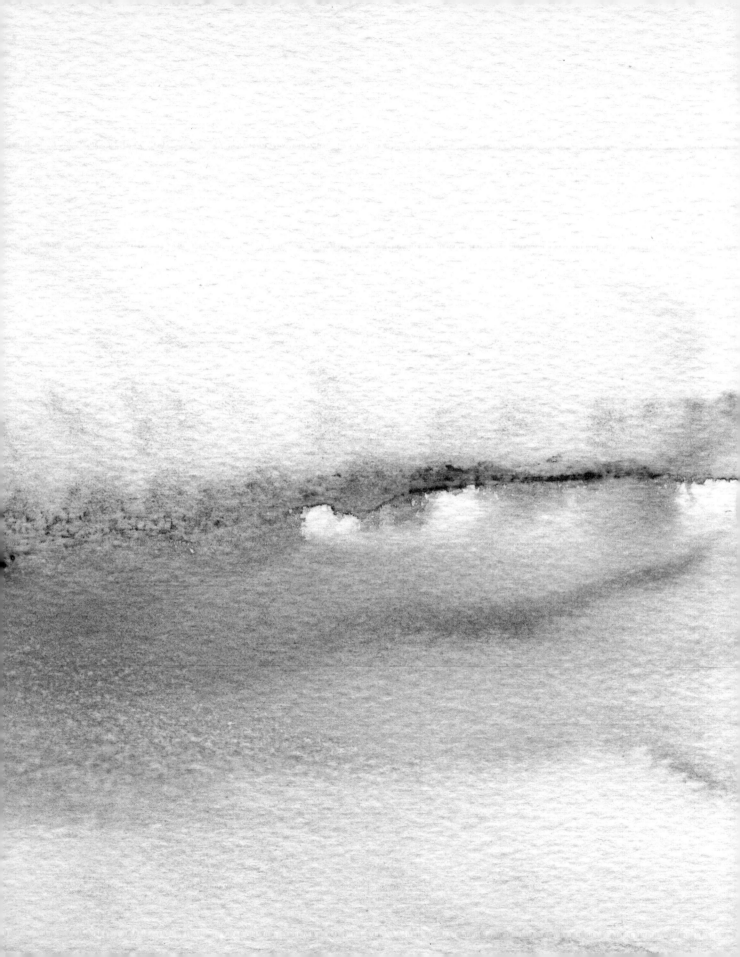